LIVING IN
Australia

LIVING IN
Australia

BETSY WALTER
JEAN WRIGHT

WITH ADDITIONAL TEXT
BY MOIRA MAGUIRE

Chronicle Books • San Francisco

First published in the United States in 1992 by Chronicle Books

Copyright © Kevin Weldon & Associates Pty Limited 1991

Library of Congress Cataloging in Publication Data available

Printed in Singapore

ISBN 0-8118-0139-X

Distributed in Canada by Raincoast Books
112 Third Avenue, Vancouver, B.C. V5T 1C8

10 9 8 7 6 5 4 3 2 1

Chronicle Books
275 Fifth Street
San Francisco, CA 94103

ACKNOWLEDGMENTS

The authors would like to thank all those whose special efforts, support and particular wisdom made the difference.

To the Sydney marketing unit of KPMG Peat Marwick and the staff of *Belle* magazine for their encouragement and sustaining friendship; to Harry and Penelope Seidler for their ever-open door, and for opening many other doors; to Robin Duffecy, Stephanie King and Maria Jenkins for help when it counted most; to Clive Lucas for being a splendid source and resource; to Julia Richardson for giving up all those weekends; to Margie Bromilow for inspiration and encouragement; to Janne Faulkner and Harley Anstee of Nexus Designs for their many contributions from earliest days to the eleventh hour; to Margot Montgomery, Appley Hoare, Geoffrey Clarke, Gregory Ford, Sheila Carroll, Robert Grant and Murray Collins for location suggestions; to Carolyn Lockhart and Joan Bowers for their help on Broome; to *Vogue Living*, Victoria Alexander, Christine Whiston, Piero Gesualdi, Vincent Interlandi, Nicholas Bochsler, Allen Jack & Cottier, and McIntyre Partnership for their generous supply of transparencies; to Mary Larnach-Jones for her photographs of Sanders Wood; to Pamela Bell for her invaluable advice on Queensland properties; to Palms of the World proprietors Mike and Catharina Kenny and the Carter family for their hospitality at Mission Beach; to Pamela Croci, Derek Scott and Jane Whitehouse for critical props; to Christine Daly and Heidi Crosweller for their able and willing assistance; and to Australian Airlines' Martin Kelly, Yolande Rademaker and Amanda Gregory for getting us where we had to go. Finally, we are especially grateful to all the owners who generously allowed us to photograph their homes, and to the photographers — as always, our closest collaborators.

For our editor, Annette Carter, whose life was taken over by this book for the better part of a year and whose extraordinary efforts and ability brought it to fruition, mere thanks can never be enough.

PHOTOGRAPHIC CREDITS

All photographs, *except those indicated by italics*, are copyright © Weldon Trannies. The endpapers feature a detail of a silk scarf by Jenny Kee.

Allen Jack & Cottier, 68 (top); M. Bianchino, 25 (bottom, left); Anthony Browell, 4–5, 138–43; Kevin Burchett, 25 (top, left and right; centre, left); *Jo Daniell, 6–7; John Callanan (courtesy of Victoria Alexander), 260–3, 270*; Earl Carter, 2–3, 22 (top, right), 30–5, 132–6, 150–61, 176–81, 200–3, 258; Michelle Darlington, 25 (bottom, right); Philip Fischer (endpapers); *Robert Gray/AusChromes, 241; Grant Hancock/Jaisay Pty Ltd, 188–91*; John Hay, 12, 52–3, 64–7, 78–85, 106–13, 244 (bottom, left and right), 245–9, *254–6, 257 (bottom)*; Ray Joyce, 18–19, 22 (left, and two at centre right), 23, 104, 162–6, 196–9, 214–19, 220–5, 226, 228–37; Neil Lorimer, *36–9 (courtesy of Vincent Interlandi)*, 44–7, 120–3, *182–7, 268–9*; Geoff Lung, 48–51, 68 (bottom), 69–73, 96–103, 114–19, 144–9, 168–75, 192–5; *McIntyre Partnership, 257 (top)*; M. McLeod, 24 (centre); I. R. Marriner, 17; Leo Meier, 21 (bottom), 24 (bottom), 25 (centre, right), 28, 62; *Mirage Gold Coast Management Pty Ltd and Desmond Brooks International Pty Ltd, 238, 240, 242–3; Fran Moore, 244 (top); Nexus Designs Pty Limited, 250–3*; Stephen Nutt, 20; Andrew Payne, 26, 40–3, 44–7, 54–5, 62, 74–7, 86–91, 124–5, 126 (top); *Diana Petruccelli (courtesy of Piero Gesualdi), 266–7*; Larry Phillips, 24 (top); *Harry Seidler, 92–5; Eric Sierins, 126 (bottom), 127*; Tim Vanderlaan, 15; *Vogue Living (© The Condé Nast Publications Pty Limited), 128–31 (Rodney Weidland), 264–5 (Anthony Browell)*; Rodney Weidland, 22 (bottom, right), 56–61, 204–13; Weldon Trannies, 15, 16 (except bottom, left), 21; *Wildlight Photo Agency/Philip Quirk, 16 (centre, right, and bottom, left)*.

C O N T E N T S

As BIG BILL NEIDJIE OF THE Gagudju people has said, "Our story is in the land . . . it is written in those sacred places . . . you can't change it, no matter who you are." These words mean a lot to me. They sum up my strongest feelings about this country. My deep love for Australia really only began when I returned home after living in London for seven years during the 1960s. Having grown up in Bondi, I had always taken for granted the qualities that make Australia so different from other parts of the world: the intense light and the vast expanses of colour. And until then I had never really appreciated the timelessness of the Australian landscape: the fact that it had existed much as it is today long before humans came to tame it and that it would endure long after we were gone. It was this realization of the strength and uniqueness of Australia that filled me with an urgent need to try to capture these special qualities and to pioneer a style that reflected them.

Australian style suggests many images to me. It's the rainbow colours of rosellas and parrots as they flash through a bush garden; it's waking to the laughter of kookaburras at dawn; it's the sensuous trunks of silver gums, and kangaroos nibbling clover on the lawn at sunset; it's the weathered ochre of ancient Aboriginal rock paintings in a remote outback cave; it's the feel of hot sand under your feet at the beach in summer. But it's also the Sydney Harbour Bridge and the Opera House, those two magnificent monuments to man's creative energy.

In this country we are surrounded by colour — strong colour and strong sun. I see colour as being related to optimism, and I see Australians as a strong, spontaneous, bold and optimistic people. More and more, we are learning to listen to the voice of nature, to make friends with the landscape and not to feel threatened by it, and this feeling is being reflected in the work of our architects and designers.

Australian style can be expressed in many different ways, but there is a common thread running through them all. Above all, Australian style is about feeling free and open to life.

JENNY KEE

Jenny Kee is a Sydney-based designer.

[LEFT] *Individually hand-painted chairs add a touch of fantasy to a fashionable Melbourne house.*

Australia possesses not one style, but many. It is a modern nation spread out across an ancient land. It is a place of formal contrasts and contradictions: oppositions of size and population; Aboriginal and European, city and country, beliefs and needs; the dialectics of poetic and pragmatic values.

To understand Australia is to know the history of its colonial beginnings and social progress; of land tenure, pastoral and industrial activity; and, importantly, of the urban form of our beach-head capital cities. What is really critical to the Australian psyche is the feeling of being on the *edge* of western civilization rather than in the *centre*. This independence has done more to shape our experience than any other factor, be it attachment to landscape or awareness of Aboriginal origins.

Yet a vision of Australian centrality continues to persist: a national identity with coherent recognizable characteristics is one of the dreams that is actually a reality. Meet Australians anywhere, and in an instant you get to know about it: their key points of physical attachment to place, as well as a sense of belonging. How else can you explain the general desire to excel in all sports, and the distinguished creative abilities of individuals in arts and literature, film making, architecture and design? But Australians can also delight in a laconic sense of fun, and the ironic wit of the larrikin outsider is part of the national character.

These are the sentiments that bind. They can be recognized across the 4300 kilometres of inhospitable eroded desert that separate Darwin from Perth, as well as up and down an incredibly handsome and fertile Pacific coast which stretches as beach and bush from Tasmania to Cape York.

Designers in all disciplines now have to address a diverse spectrum of ideas and attitudes — public and private, from peripheral to purposeful argument — all shaped by the forces of inherited intellectual heritage being applied in a virgin land with unique flora and fauna, beach and bush. As a symbolic language, Australian style operates as a series of complementary layers, with aesthetic choice (like or dislike) formed through associational interpretation and imagery. One aspect of complementarity is the much-heralded attachment to "the bush" as romantic ideal. Another (equally as important) exists in the urban texts of the capital cities.

Visitors are genuinely impressed to find Australian cities of solidity and physical strength that exude civilized presence. Botanical gardens, town halls, art centres, thoughtful academic institutions, and lively and distinctive inner-urban streets of specialty shopping, cinemas and restaurants are further indicators of metropolitan panache.

Life in the country demands another form of truth: rough but real. The climate is unforgiving, unpredictable and uneven. Drought followed by flood, interspersed with fires of immense ferocity, have made their mark on the desires, and the perceptions. There is a heroism about the bush (as well as a survival instinct) that has affected our behaviour and created, through art and literature, the romantic view of a majority who prefer to live as a micro-squattocracy on quarter-acre suburban blocks: half city, half bush. This house-and-garden style represents a mediocre but substantive approximation of a supposedly individual way of life, made feasible by two cars and the freeway.

But the worth of the city as a place of purposive, technological culture directed towards the synthetic remains largely unsung in Australian mythology, or at least goes unnoticed because it is considered less exotic than similar cultural developments elsewhere. Yet, in spite of a relatively small population, Australia has always possessed a modern attitude towards style as a form of exploration and inquiry — there to be tested and changed as each new discovery is made.

Designers now are in constant dialogue with their counterparts in many other countries, and it would be wrong to suggest that design in the late twentieth century, in a technologically equipped and intelligent Australia, exists without such exchange or awareness. Australians have to encounter the world beyond their island-continent secure in the knowledge of their identity but aware of Australia's interdependence with other places; our real task is to continue to manufacture the difference. It would be foolish to try to extend these ideas further, for the text and pictures in this book illustrate the case very well.

In summary, significant Australian style may be found in the hard-won practicality of the bush, the metropolitanism of the inner city, the languid torpor of the suburb and, above all, in the naked egalitarian splendour of the beach. Australian style now is not about either the city or the bush, but rather the fertility of their combination and the real joy that attaches to the idea of incompleteness.

DARYL JACKSON, AO, FRAIA, Hon. FAIA

For Robert William Spitzer and Cicely Victoria Wright and the memory of Hubert John Wright and Elizabeth Underwood Spitzer.

And to Babette Hayes, who taught a generation of design journalists the meaning of Australian style.

NOTHING IS MORE DECEPTIVE than the surface realities of Australian style. Australians are quite happy to meet popular perceptions head-on, to produce Crocodile Dundees, didgeridoos and Drizabones on demand, concealing the true complexity of Australian life from casual visitors who expect a kind of culturally curious Eden. Why disappoint them?

The comfortable frontier, the Italians call it. Yet Australia is much more aware of the world than the world is aware of Australia. Australian style, in all its urban, suburban and country variations, forms through the interplay of international influences its own complex multiculture and the perverse individuality of an island-continent where birds laugh, and mammals lay eggs, and everything familiar is somehow altered, suddenly unique.

For better or for worse, Australia has developed through the imposition of European cultures on a vast continent inhabited by an Aboriginal people, whose sensitive and delicate occupation of the land was no match for western traditions of possession. But the land itself has been more than a match for the new arrivals. The driest continent, yet capable of savage transformation, Australia is given to violent and sudden storms, fire, hail, drought and flood. In the year this book was put together, an area of grazing land the size of Europe lay under water while elsewhere the land lay parched in drought, hailstones the size of golf balls fell on Melbourne, and a cyclone ripped apart the Sydney suburb of Turramurra.

As the land reaches up periodically to smite the overconfident and to humble the elaborately stylish, humour is not far from the surface of Australian design. There is an easy, unforced informality about much of the current design work that comes too from the benign aspects of a land that lies under the equator. The climate is moderate and the land open and generous — if occasionally hostile. It is also distant from old traditions and constrictions. One can, within reason, do what one likes.

One of Australia's great wellsprings of style has been the displacement in space from its western heritage. Australia is simply too far away from its cultural roots to participate in a constant stylistic dialogue with Europe and North America; it has been forced to find and develop, and now delights in, its own language of

[LEFT] *The quintessentially Australian greeting finds structural expression in the G'Day chair, designed by Brian Sayer, the letters of the word forming the back and legs.*

13

style. Beginning with honest mills and simple shearing sheds, the Australian tradition of adaptation came to town, and it has never left. And from the sombre respectability of high Victoriana, architects and designers have acted, reacted, adapted and forged ahead towards a contemporary style which, like the Mediterranean, accepts the sun and the light as our natural inheritance.

Artists and designers visiting Australia for the first time are struck by the light, which has a special quality uncommon (if not unknown) in Europe and North America: clear, hard, laser-intense by day, and gauzily pastel at dusk. With this light comes a relentless heat which bears down on pavements and paddocks alike. Australian buildings, whether they are part of an inner-city cluster or solitary in the outback, respond to this light, forming shelter for lazy afternoons and shielding windows. And just as children stand at the beach, so the boundary space between inside and out — the verandah — forms the basis for much of Australia's architectural imagery and outdoor life.

Australia began in the Anglo-Irish tradition, but what was born as an English penal colony has evolved into a multicultural land of opportunity. The layers of diversity that now come under the umbrella of Australian style owe their richness to this country's many national groups, where elements of Europe and Asia are distilled and decanted into something undeniably and peculiarly Australian.

Australia, then, is no monoculture, but a forerunner of things to come. It is post-1992 Europe and the Asian Common Market all rolled into one. Such diversity can be seen in America, but Australia has no supervening white sauce to smother the lot. The ingredients are there for us to see and savour, the rough edges and the humour visible to all.

ROGER POOLE, FRAIA

Director, Bates, Smart & McCutcheon

BETSY WALTER

TIME AND WEATHER LEAVE NO LASTING IMPRINT ON THE MIGHTY OCEAN AT Australia's door, nor on the vast red emptiness at her heart, but they deeply etch their passage on all things manmade. The struggle and celebration of living in this cruel, exhilarating land is a story told in wide arcs of sandy beaches bathed in blinding light, in the glint of iron and the strange perfume of eucalypts, in the landlocked driftwood of a solitary outback cottage and the rhythms of lacework on inner-city terrace houses.

Early Australian architecture was loosely based on contemporary British trends, with a local flavour starting to be introduced by the necessity to build quickly and with whatever materials were at hand. By the end of the nineteenth century, an Australian vernacular style had begun to appear, especially in country areas, where external influences and fashions had least impact.

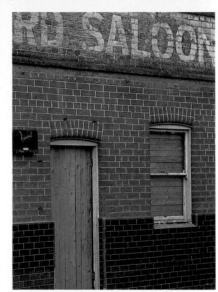

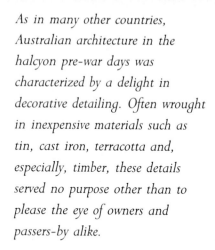

As in many other countries, Australian architecture in the halcyon pre-war days was characterized by a delight in decorative detailing. Often wrought in inexpensive materials such as tin, cast iron, terracotta and, especially, timber, these details served no purpose other than to please the eye of owners and passers-by alike.

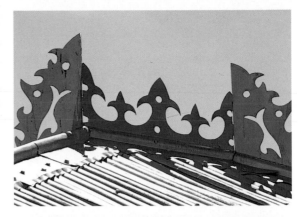

OONOORABA

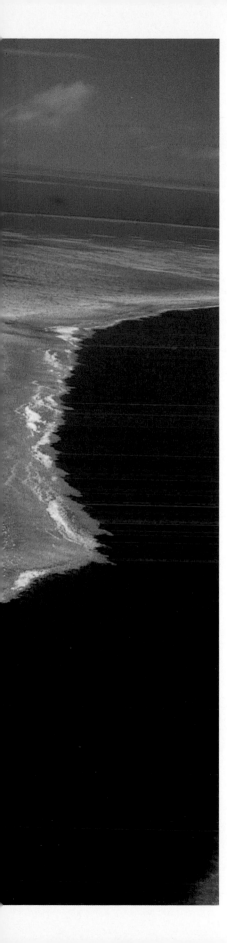

Australia is the most urbanized country in the world, with the highest percentage of its population living in cities. This leaves a lot of the "island continent" only sparsely populated, and most Australians, including those living in the cities, think of their land as one of wide, open spaces.

Whether it's the vast expanse of the Great Barrier Reef, the seemingly endless desert punctuated by the remarkable Ayers Rock, or fields of pasture either glistening in the sun or covered in snow, Australia's landscapes are as extensive as they are varied.

21

If there is one element that encapsulates Australian style, it's the verandah. Whether it's overlooking endless pastures or the street and neighbours, the verandah has been the place to sit out of the sun, to chat with friends and family, or simply to contemplate the world ever since the early farmers first surrounded their English-influenced, Georgian-style homes with a shelter of timber and corrugated iron.

23

Early Australian architecture often featured shades of brown, green and yellow, or simply left materials such as timber in their natural state. More recently, appreciation of the landscape is often reflected by using expanses of single colours as bold and as lively as the sky, the seas and the fields.

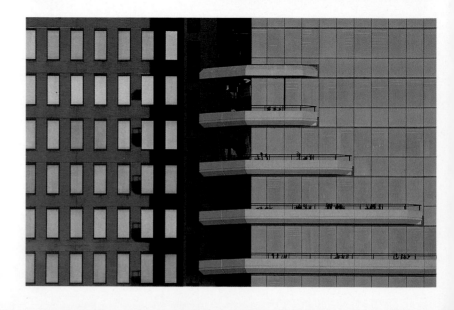

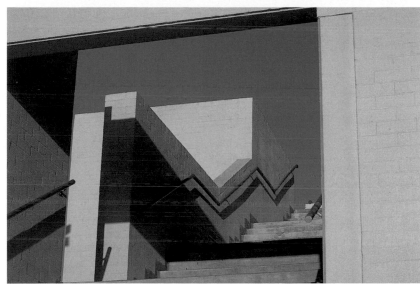

A<small>USTRALIANS ARE AN URBAN</small>
people with a wilderness sensibility. Most of us live in dense capital-city clusters
at the edge of the sea, no strangers to skylines bristling with skyscrapers, yet we
cleave to the images of the bush — if not the Australian bush, then the weathered
patinas of the Italian *campagna* and the French *village*. And we are a people quite
capable of resolving the incongruities between high-density living and an affinity
with sunlight. City style is about that resolution.

Deep in the inner-city suburbs, we have taken our old Victorian terraces and
cottages with their backs to the sun, and opened them into garden courtyards. We
value space indoors and exterior space, and we prize those apartments that offer
decks and roof gardens, not just ornamental architectural trim. Beyond the dense
urban fabric, our suburban houses may provide only marginally more outdoor
living area, but we have learned how to extract the maximum yield from every
sunlit centimetre, and how to gather that light and space and direct them within.

Above all, city style is also about the Australian sensibility. When there is
formality, there is also humour. Where there is a statement of high style, there is
also the throwaway line. The best of Australian urban design makes no claims to
the ultra-chic, the ultra-grand or the ultra-luxurious. It stakes out its territory in
the sunlight, where pretensions wither and invention takes root.

27

[LEFT] *The view from this
harbourside apartment
takes in the splendid
sweep of Rushcutters Bay,
with the blue-ribbon
eastern suburb of Darling
Point beyond.*

TERRACES & COTTAGES

As architecturally emblematic of Sydney as the Harbour Bridge or the Opera House — although by no means unique to that city — the terrace house of the Victorian era gives rhythm to the city's residential streetscapes, tracing in its rows the rise and fall of the hilly terrain and the serpentine vagaries of its streets.

In all its variations — grand, humble, wide, narrow, adorned with elaborate traceries of cast iron, or plain-faced — the terrace is an urban creation designed to live side by side with neighbouring counterparts. In the manner of its cousins, the Manhattan brownstone and the London row house, and like its relative, the Sydney cottage, it is most pleasing to the eye when seen in multiples of a single theme.

The answer to an exploding demand for inner-city housing after the Gold Rush, the terrace house lost its cachet with the advent of the garden suburb in 1900, but returned to favour with a vengeance in the late 1960s as the voguish residence for the urban arts-and-letters set. Today, terrace dwellers are not so homogeneously categorized, but the faint air of association between the avant-garde and the city terrace still lingers.

Many terrace and cottage owners share the problem of the old "tunnel-back" configuration, an ungainly graduation of kitchen, bathroom and laundry facilities into the back garden. The most widespread solution has been to replace the rear of the house entirely, with combined kitchen/entertaining rooms opening out onto a garden courtyard. With this resolution, the results are unendingly varied and delightful.

[LEFT] *Rows of Victorian terraces are the hallmark of Sydney's inner suburbs and are synonymous with Paddington.*

29

COUNTRY STYLE, CITY CHIC

Living above the store has taken on a new connotation for antiques expert and interior designer John Normyle and his wife, florist Alison Coates. The couple live and work in two adjoining early village shops in Sydney's Paddington. One half of the ground floor is given over to Mr Normyle's country-style furniture, primitive and religious figurines, old musical instruments and ancient terracotta pots, the other to Alison Coates's flower shop. But distinctions between the two shops are blurred; even in the flower shop it's easy to collide with the odd Roman pillar or trip over a Greek statue.

Mr Normyle's eye is for the rough-hewn items of the *campagna*—far more suitable to the Australian climate, he believes, than the Victoriana that dominates so many terrace houses. In the flower shop, rich tan walls match the oiled waxed paper used for wrapping informal bouquets tied with baler's twine that Ms Coates dyes herself. Containers range from primitive African baskets and old limewashed pots to Spanish terracotta oil jars and unpainted tin pails.

Everything in the house/shops is for sale. Both dealers are quite used to emptying wardrobes and drawers, even removing flowers from the washing basket. And when it gets to the point that they have to sit on the floor for lunch, Mr Normyle and Ms Coates simply go to Spain.

[ABOVE] *Looking from the Normyle shop through to Ms Coates's florist shop. An eighteenth-century Spanish table is complemented by a chestnut cupboard of the same period. To the left is a painted wooden head of a saint.*

[RIGHT] *A Paddington vignette: designer/antiques dealer John Normyle in front of his furniture shop, and florist Alison Coates amid her arrangements. The couple live and work in a pair of terrace houses joined inside, where the distinction between shops—and between home and office space—is often blurred. Above the flower shop and off the balcony is the dining room.*

Mr Normyle's upstairs work area, looking
through to the dining room. The blue
balustrade, partly visible at right, was removed
from the terrace's narrow stairway and now
decorates the stairwell wall.

[ABOVE, LEFT] *Design plans and drawings are stored in terracotta jars on an old Spanish corner table. The Dujong figurine is from Africa.*

[ABOVE, CENTRE] *A country chair with rush seat blends beautifully with the old waxed floorboards and the bright yellow balcony door.*

[ABOVE, RIGHT] *Lunch, Mediterranean-style, is a daily Normyle specialty prepared for "anyone who happens to be around".*

[LEFT] *In the dining room, rush-covered chairs are gathered around an iron French bistro table topped with a huge vase of waratahs from Alison Coates's shop. Against one wall an old school drum balances on a cupboard made from lengths of timber.*

[ABOVE] *An array of useful implements, balsamic vinegar and a cappuccino-maker line the wall of the stove alcove in the upstairs kitchen.*

[RIGHT] *Looking past a collection of Normyle antiques through to the kitchen. An old Spanish dresser and simple rush-covered chairs contrast with the streamlined kitchen workbench.*

The corner kitchen, squeezed into a small space upstairs, features a narrow sink, stove and workbench trimmed top and bottom in stainless steel. Overhead, a knife from a French advertising display hangs like the sword of Damocles above the benchtop.

The Interlandis' attached cottage is one in a row of typical inner-city dwellings of the Victorian period. Variously referred to as single-fronted or workmen's cottages, these houses were designed for the working classes.

POST-MODERN REVAMP

As the price of inner-city housing escalates, so too does the popularity of the old — and relatively inexpensive — single-fronted workman's cottage. The challenge for renovators is to work within the restrictions of long narrow corridors, and rooms only 4 metres wide, and to resolve the now-undesirable Victorian layout of streetfront parlour and rear kitchen/laundry that turns its back on the garden.

Architect Vincent Interlandi and his wife, Lydia, have approached their redesign of a single-storey terrace house in Melbourne with colour and deconstructed cut-out dynamism, not so much reinventing the layout as resurfacing the Victoriana with a contemporary sensibility.

The given floor plan — a long, narrow corridor with two rooms on one side and opening into a central room — has been retained, but now the plane of the corridor wall leaps out into three dimensions with a storm-blue modular overlay. The walls of the front study, dining room and kitchen are intact but highly coloured, with chrome-yellow and blue surfaces generating a powerful visual dynamic within otherwise ordinary spaces.

Like most newly renovated terraces and cottages, the Interlandi house now turns its back on the street, reoriented towards the privacy and greenery of a rear garden with a new entertaining/sitting area opening onto the outdoors through floor-to-ceiling glass doors. A handsome ash floor inlaid with jarrah links the procession of rooms, binding the design together with a sophisticated "fifth wall" that, like the rest of this post-Modern revamp, would have astonished the builders of this once-humble little house.

37

[ABOVE AND LEFT] *The long side passage of the interior, a standard feature of the single-fronted cottage, has been given a visually dynamic 3-D treatment of colour and modular shaping.*

[RIGHT] *Chrome yellow and stormy blue walls create a visual break between study, dining room and kitchen.*

[BELOW, LEFT] *A downlit vase of flowers adds drama and dimension to the compact interior.*

[BELOW, CENTRE] *Cut-outs in the wall of the small study provide a whimsical view of the rooms to the rear of the house.*

[BELOW, RIGHT] *A traditional dining room setting with tapestry upholstery contrasts with the post-Modern architectural additions.*

[OPPOSITE PAGE] *Typical of the current approach to Victorian cottage renovations, the rear of the house has been converted into a private living area flowing into a courtyard.*

MEDITERRANEAN AT HEART

This charming turn-of-the-century cottage in Sydney's Bellevue Hill suffered many indignities until rescued by Vikki Ross. Renovating the "already-renovated" involved much work and not a little heartache, including the constant supervision of a wistaria vine forced to spend a year flat on the ground awaiting the construction of a new pergola.

The hub of the house is now the large Mediterranean-style living/dining room, whose tiled floor and French doors visually and physically link the interior with the rear garden. Here the precious wistaria now tumbles over a fine timber pergola, creating a springtime extravaganza of blossom, then cool summer shade for an outdoor room where Ms Ross entertains at a long table. It is a perfect setting for a casual luncheon or a candlelit dinner.

The kitchen is a town version of country style, with brick cupboards finished in Tasmanian oak, open shelves, and blue and white French tiles on walls and splashback. The blue and white theme is continued in the bathroom, where a deep Roman bath and the basin have been edged with Italian border tiles.

Animals are a big part of Ms Ross's life. During the renovations her white pony enjoyed a sabbatical in the back garden while bantams wandered in and out of the house at will—their favourite perch the kitchen windowsill.

[ABOVE] *French doors allow a flood of light into the bathroom from the side passage. Blue and white French floor tiles from Pazotti in Sydney were teamed with Italian border tiles for a country effect.*

[RIGHT] *Terracatto walls and painted full-length shutters suggest a Mediterranean-inspired interior behind the traditional double-fronted cottage facade.*

[ABOVE] *Bantam hens roosting on a kitchen windowsill are not exactly a typical scene in Sydney's fashionable eastern suburbs, but then Vikki's pony was spelled in the back garden for a time, too.*

[LEFT] *The rustic kitchen features brick cupboards with Tasmanian oak doors and open board shelving.*

[RIGHT] *Looking through the large rear living room to the gently upward-sloping garden.*

[FAR RIGHT] *The table set for a midsummer's Sunday party.*

[BELOW] *A sweep of diagonally laid terracotta tiles cover the renovated living/entertaining area at the rear. Bagged walls were finished in a red-oxide-tinted plaster applied with a plastering brush. Adding his own solid presence to the strong look of the English furniture is Zimmer, a Keeshond.*

42

[OPPOSITE PAGE] *Entertaining well is a part of the Ross household routine. The pergola and its carefully preserved wistaria vine provide a dappled outdoor setting for a smartly laid table.*

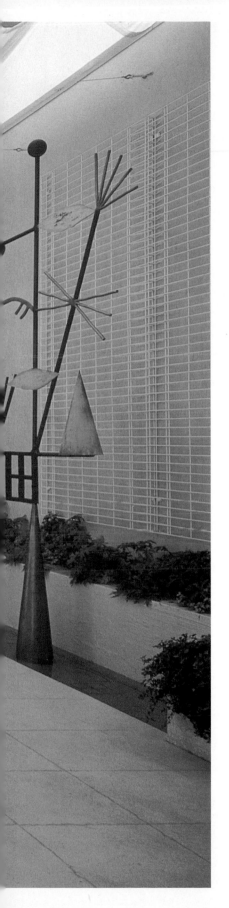

[LEFT] The Italianate exterior of Janne Faulkner's grand Melbourne terrace. Dating from the 1880s, Mount Erina's facade has been classified by the National Trust of Victoria.

[OPPOSITE PAGE] A white concertinaed canvas awning shades the courtyard, accessible from the living room, kitchen and bedroom areas. A Peter Cole sculpture specially commissioned by the owner was installed in the small mosaic-lined pool.

A TERRACE IN THE GRAND MANNER

Designer Janne Faulkner's city home is one of the few Italianate villas in the Melbourne suburb of South Yarra. Dating from the late nineteenth century, they represent a boom time for the colony, when European, rather than purely British, influences became part of Australian architecture.

Little now remains of the original house except its magnificent facade, which has been classified by the National Trust, and two highly decorated ceilings. To preserve the architectural features yet make it practical for contemporary owners, the house was gutted and restructured to create two spaces, one for living and another for cooking. An additional area of three squares was built, providing a bedroom, dressing room and bathroom, and all three areas were opened into a northern courtyard. By using glass doors to integrate the courtyard with the interior and painting its walls in the same colour, Ms Faulkner removed the usual visual indoor/outdoor barrier.

[RIGHT] *Behind Mount Erina's classical facade there lies a modern heart, with polished terrazzo floors and contemporary chairs. Floor-to-ceiling bookshelves flank the blank-walled fireplace, and Oriental carpets and cream walls add depth and richness to the interior.*

[BELOW, LEFT] *Cupboards were finished in a soft grey as a contrast to the cream walls. Stools tucked beneath the bench create a breakfast bar. Double doors lead out to the courtyard.*

[BELOW, RIGHT] *A highly ornate ceiling sets off the streamlined finishes of the kitchen, with its sleek units, terrazzo benchtops and contemporary paintings.*

46

Like the kitchen, the guest bedroom boasts an ornate ceiling, in contrast to the rest of the house, where designer Janne Faulkner opted for minimalism. The ceiling and walls are finished in a paint palette of graduated cream shades, creating an old-lace effect overhead.

MODERN CLASSIC

Built in the heart of Sydney's Paddington, this new addition to the terrace-and-lace streetscape of the neighbourhood is "a building that councils and anyone interested in the revitalization of inner-city areas should look closely at", according to the judges who gave it the 1988 Robin Boyd Award for Residential Works.

Architect Alex Tzannes also captured the prized Wilkinson Award for this superb infill home, the first in a series of what eventually will be five buildings that take their historical cues from townhouses in New York, London and Rome, and can claim a conceptual pedigree going back to Palladio.

Like its historical antecedents, the Henwood house is finely balanced and handsomely proportioned, an elegant stand-alone design that also fits in well with its neighbours without copying them. A full three storeys high in a street of two-storey terraces, it conforms to the street's sightlines, its parapet level with that of the terrace next door.

48

[ABOVE, LEFT] *Clean lines of furniture and interior space maximize the sense of space and refinement in the living area.*

[ABOVE, RIGHT] *Like traditional Paddington terraces, the house graduates from its broad street facade to a pleasing scale of smaller architectural masses at the rear.*

[RIGHT] *Distinct from, but in harmony with, its Victorian neighbours, the Henwood house does not interrupt the rhythms of the Paddington terrace streetscape.*

*Outside the living area, a tailored courtyard
sandwiched between the main building and the
garage provides a private space for outdoor
entertaining and relaxing, sheltered from the
activity of the Paddington streets beyond.*

Looking from the dining area to the living area. The wide square arch and columns define space without encroaching on it. Brushbox flooring is a rich counterpoint to the simple interior finish.

A small draped table softens the formality of the columned arch and creates a decorative baffle in the otherwise-transparent space between the corridor and the living area. To the right is the entry to the kitchen.

A central skylit stair creates a lightwell in the heart of the Henwood house, an inclusion that judges for the 1988 Robin Boyd Award for Residential Works found "astonishing", given the small size of the site.

The central glass skylight gable seen from the top floor of the three-storey house. A charming passage-cum-balcony connects the interior spaces around the lightwell.

PADDINGTON PALLADIAN

This Paddington house is the second in what will be architect Alex Tzannes' series of five Palladian-inspired designs for inner-Sydney living. Like the first house in the series — the Henwood house shown on the preceding pages — this elegantly wrought house has been honoured by the Royal Australian Institute of Architects at both state and national levels.

Like the Henwood house, the house is a remarkable example of what can be extracted from a small inner-city site, a mere 6 metre by 36 metre plot. And where its Victorian terrace neighbours contain only two storeys, Tzannes has managed four, including a basement, without exploding out of scale with the adjoining row of buildings. At the heart of the design is the double-volume living area, intersected with a staircase laid crossways to the house, freeing up the limited width of the internal space.

[ABOVE] *The ground-level entry walkway overlooks the double-height living area below, and leads to a study on the same floor.*

[RIGHT] *Positioned crossways to the house, rather than down its length (as in conventional terrace layouts), the staircase zigzags through vertical space, leaving the 6 metre width of the house uninterrupted and accentuating the double-volume height of the basement living and entertaining area.*

[OPPOSITE PAGE, LEFT] *A stepped and balconied design at the rear of the house provides outdoor areas overlooking the courtyard for the upper levels.*

[OPPOSITE PAGE, RIGHT] *For a city house, outdoor space is plentiful here, with all rooms leading to a courtyard or balcony. In keeping with the spirit of the architecture, the owners have adopted an uncluttered casual chic style of decorating. The white canvas-covered sofa sits well on the deep natural shade of the brushbox boards.*

53

STREET SMART

Victorian terrace houses in their original state are typically dark, with small rooms and a layout ill suited to today's lifestyles. Purists will argue that they should be left that way, but most terrace owners prefer to adapt them to take in more sun and to create a better spatial flow.

Sydney publicist Marita Blood changed hers twice before she had what she really wanted — an open-plan, light-filled living area and kitchen which flows out to the garden, and the bedrooms, television room, office and bathroom upstairs. From the front door, visitors now enter a huge main room, deliberately flamboyant in style, with Italian chandeliers and French chairs.

A pine table, teamed with ten Italian wrought-iron chairs, dominates the kitchen and is complemented by a huge amphora and a Spanish cupboard, which stand either side of the kitchen's old fireplace.

[ABOVE, LEFT] *Marita Blood's 120-year-old terrace house is one of a row of terraces in a fashionable Woollahra street. Like many terrace houses in Sydney's near-city suburbs, its exterior has been left unrenovated to avoid attracting the attention of would-be thieves.*

[ABOVE, RIGHT] *To one side of the living room fireplace, a campaign chair is teamed with an old Australian table and a still life of flowers.*

[RIGHT] *The master bedroom has a simple all-white theme, complete with white-painted floorboards. The collapsible campaign chairs were made in Australia.*

[ABOVE AND LEFT] *An early Australian pine table is the centrepiece of the large eat-in kitchen. Teamed with ten Italian wrought-iron chairs, it contributes to the ambience of elegant simplicity. An old Spanish cupboard and a large Italian oil jar define the kitchen fireplace.*

[FAR LEFT] *A detail from the long narrow garden at the rear of the house.*

A PAINTERLY EYE

It is more than two decades since Sydney artist Margaret Olley moved into a tiny hat factory — and its adjoining terrace — and made it her home. The house is crammed with objects that have taken the artist's fancy: an array of bowls, plates and jugs, rich in colour; a wooden sheep adorned with Indian beads; a haphazard collection of odd chairs. Finished paintings lean against walls wherever there is space. Carved wooden figures, vases of flowers and baskets of ripe fruit cover almost every horizontal surface. The result is a melange of colour, pattern and texture, every bit as fascinating as the artist's work.

There is no studio, but her home is itself rich in subjects. Margaret Olley carries her palette from one place to the next, painting the still-life canvasses that eventually join fine art collections around the world.

Undoubtedly it is a painter's eye that has determined this interior. Side tables catch the light, mirrors reflect particular perspectives, and among the vast array of objects, one senses an underlying feeling of order, a certain placement, a way of "looking" that is reflected in Margaret Olley's work.

The artist is protective of her privacy, a fact that biographer Christine France attributes to the public furore surrounding a portrait of Olley by William Dobell, which won the 1948 Archibald Prize.

However, for those of her close friends privileged to gather around the large dining table, the Olley environment provides an ever-changing vista, the special insight of the artist's eye.

57

[ABOVE] *A comfortable sofa in the foreground and cluttered shelves beyond, evidence of the artist's belief that a house must look "lived in".*

[LEFT] *A statue of Saint Michael is one of many esoteric objects to conceal the surface of what might otherwise serve as a dining table.*

[OPPOSITE PAGE] *The world of the artist: Margaret Olley seated in the house where she has lived for more than twenty years.*

[TOP, LEFT AND RIGHT] *Margaret Olley's home is her studio, and every casually arranged collection of objects forms an intriguing still life.*

[CENTRE, LEFT] *Eastern heads and a very ordinary jug combine to create a mood of serenity.*

[CENTRE, RIGHT] *No object exists in isolation. Here, a wooden artist's model, a wicker basket and tulips make a study of contrasts.*

[RIGHT] *A garden as jumbled as the interior of the house can be seen through the long windows of the main room.*

[FAR RIGHT] *A weathered stone unicorn half-hidden underneath lavender bushes.*

[LEFT] *Dried proteas and Belgian decoy birds have been arranged inside a carved wooden niche.*

[FAR LEFT] *A wooden sheep is hung with Indian beads.*

[BELOW] *Dried flowers, carved figures and bowls of fruit in endless variations and combinations cover every surface of the two-room house.*

[RIGHT] *Olley canvasses stacked up against walls and furniture in the adjoining terrace house.*

[BELOW, LEFT] *A pair of wooden goats from Margaret Olley's collection of carved figures.*

[BELOW, RIGHT] *Light streams through a window onto a comfortable reading chair. One of the artist's paintings hangs in the background.*

[ABOVE] *A Margaret Olley painting of the* Yellow Room.

[LEFT] *The room itself. Above the mantelpiece is Matisse's* Red Room.

APARTMENTS & TOWNHOUSES

Australia's cities do not have a long tradition of apartment living. Until recent decades, units were designed primarily to accommodate two age groups: young adults on the first rung of the ladder toward house ownership, and senior citizens trading down from home ownership to units.

Over the past twenty years, strata living has become not only acceptable as a first or last home but downright fashionable — indeed, Australia's most internationally celebrated architect, Harry Seidler, built himself an ultra-glamorous penthouse atop his new office building in Sydney's Milsons Point — while townhouses, once the social inferior of the house, now claim prime waterfront positions and brilliant architecture to match.

Water views, roof decks and classic pre- and post-war architectural advantages of high ceilings and spacious rooms weigh heavily in calculating the value of an apartment. In many places, grand houses have been transformed into apartments complete with a legacy of fireplaces, ornate ceilings and cedar woodwork, while the best of the new developments reveal a concentrated effort to maximize site and view orientation, together with a new sophistication and close attention to detail that are usually reserved for the top end of the market. Most significantly of all, the ad hoc decorating of apartments in the past is now yielding to major design investment, involving the talents of architects and designers of the calibre of Furio Valich and John Normyle.

[LEFT] *Apartment blocks crowd the water's edge in Sydney's Kirribilli.*

63

TOORAK, TUSCAN-STYLE

The Tuscan influence is strong in contemporary Australian architecture. Interior designer Margie Bromilow and her husband, Marshall Grosby, have built three new townhouses in Melbourne's Toorak that look as if they have been lifted straight from a Florentine streetscape. One of these is home for them and their young son, William.

Stuccoed walls, elegant proportions, detailed mouldings around the front door, roof and windows, blue-washed accents, and shutters all reflect not only Tuscan inspiration but also authentic Italian style.

Terracotta tiles have been laid in tessellated pattern throughout the ground floor, and a wrought-iron Diego Giacometti-inspired stair rail leads from the light-flooded foyer to the first floor. Terracotta is again used for tiling in the rear courtyard, with its small central spa and wrought-iron furniture. Italian marble features strongly in bathrooms and kitchen.

[ABOVE] *The Florentine-inspired streetscape of the three Toorak townhouses built by Margie Bromilow and her husband, Marshall Grosby.*
[OPPOSITE PAGE AND LEFT] *The terracotta-tiled courtyard, with its heated spa, simple wrought-iron furniture and oversized shade umbrella. The blue-washed accents of the architectural paintwork are echoed in the blue-grey stripes of the outdoor furniture covers.*

[RIGHT] *A mirrored wall in the dining room adds visual depth to the space and provides a backdrop for a pair of elegant French chairs and the French cupboard. A collection of Japanese lacquerware rests on the sofa table at right.*

[BELOW] *In the main living area a handsome Empire mirror hangs over the fireplace. Either side are floor-to-ceiling bookcases hand-stippled by Melbourne artist Nicholas Register.*

[LEFT] *Marble was used throughout the master bathroom, which features a double-bowed twin basin unit, raised shower and bath. A cheeky "G'Day" chair (formed from these four letters) adds a touch of whimsy to the surroundings. Mirrored sliding doors lead to a dressing room.*

[FAR LEFT] *A round bedside table shows off family photos and some favourite objects, including a green glass goanna.*

Pure silk taffeta curtains were used to dress the French doors of the master bedroom. The doors open out to a wrought-iron French balcony sill.

HOLIDAY HOUSE
IN THE CITY

Take one new townhouse with a fantastic location but a ho-hum floor plan, turn the interior back to front, substitute rough materials for smooth, enlarge the windows and relocate the kitchen, and you have a holiday house on Sydney Harbour a few minutes from the city.

Located on the waterfront at Long Nose Point, Birchgrove, the townhouse is one of a row of six designed by Allen Jack & Cottier. It is built on three levels, with the main rooms facing the harbour. The owners wanted to recreate the cool, yet sophisticated ambience of their former home in Fiji, to be able to walk barefoot on smooth floors and cook in a kitchen equipped for professional chefs while friends relax nearby.

Interior designer John Normyle gave them an urban holiday house which is simple, uncluttered and tranquil. Bagged brick interior walls gave way to cool, white plaster; poured concrete floors that had been carpeted disappeared under tallowwood; bedroom windows were redesigned; and the kitchen and living areas were reversed to enhance sight-lines to the water.

[RIGHT] *The three-level townhouse seen from the waterfront. Living and kitchen areas are on the middle level, the guest rooms on the top floor and the master bedroom on the ground floor.*

[BELOW] *Detail of the raised living room. Furnishings here were kept uncluttered and to a minimum to reinforce the holiday-house feeling. A collection of plants thrives in glazed Japanese pots.*

[ABOVE] *Looking from the living room down to the kitchen/dining area. A low dividing wall encloses the living room without interfering with the views beyond.*

[RIGHT] *Reminiscent of the owners' holiday home in Fiji, the entrance features carved doors leading into an interior of cool tallowwood floors and uncluttered furnishings.*

[FAR RIGHT] *A wall of outsized shelves makes a big statement, complementing the equally outsized coffee table. Beyond, a sun trap admits generous amounts of filtered natural light and air.*

[RIGHT] *Looking out from the verandah across Sydney Harbour.*

[BELOW, LEFT] *Detail of the Spanish cupboard, revealing shelves deep enough to store stools.*

[BELOW, RIGHT] *A French fishmonger's table is the centrepiece of the kitchen/dining area, and against one wall is an antique Spanish cupboard painted dark green.*

[ABOVE, TOP] *A model sailing ship built in Williamstown, Melbourne, c. 1925.*

[LEFT AND ABOVE] *The brasserie-style kitchen gleams with stainless steel. Below the bench, commercial refrigerators and freezers, a marble pastry block and a chromed-steel baker's rack indicate that this is a kitchen for serious cooks. Another antique Spanish cupboard, this one painted red, features a latticed front.*

[RIGHT AND OPPOSITE PAGE] *The ground-level master bedroom opens directly into the garden. Before John Normyle's redesign, existing windows had to be closed at night for security reasons, cutting off the view. Now fitted and extended with plantation shutters, the bedroom can be open to the air and light twenty-four hours a day.*

A cool, calm setting was created for the master bathroom, with curved tub and pedestal basin. Tucked behind their own privacy screen are the loo and the shower. Modern torchères *provide a flattering light.*

URBAN OASIS

Sydneysiders place a high premium on outdoor space. Where that space is in short supply — as is usually the case with apartments and townhouses — dwellings with oversized terraces or garden plots are considered ultra-prime properties, particularly when harbour views are part of the scenery.

This harbourside townhouse enjoys both a huge terrace and a splendid view over Rushcutters Bay, and its owner has capitalized on both, turning the terrace into a stylish, inviting, Mediterranean-style garden. Close attention to the design layout on the terrace, which wraps around three sides of the structure, has transformed the space into an additional entertaining room. Potted trees and Murraya hedges frame and define areas of the terrace, and engender a welcoming sense of seclusion and tranquillity. On the sun-soaked eastern side, the owner and his guests can stretch out on timber deckchairs overlooking the harbour. Haddonstone tiles and box trees in terracotta pots provide a touch of Tuscany.

Towards the rear, a large calico awning stretches across the balcony, forming a shaded courtyard where the owner has installed a lap pool. The pool takes up only a small area, yet caters for serious swimming with a constant water current.

[ABOVE] *The balcony wraps around three sides of the townhouse. At one end, an ornamental peacock stands near a Murraya hedge.*

[RIGHT] *It is the fine attention to detail that makes the apartment such an exceptional example of interior design. Here, a painted Regency chair stands in front of Italian-strung Bennison curtains.*

[OPPOSITE PAGE] *The townhouse overlooks Rushcutters Bay in Sydney Harbour. Haddonstone tiles and terracotta pots give the apartment a Mediterranean ambience.*

[RIGHT] *A courtyard at the back of the townhouse features a small lap pool.*

[FAR RIGHT] *A double row of potted lemon trees lines the walls to the pool.*

[BELOW] *The Lutyens bench and table, made by Australian Timber Products, provide a stylish setting for outdoor dining.*

[OPPOSITE PAGE] *The balcony is used as an extra room in this harbourside apartment. Calico awnings and a high wall spilling over with jasmine protect the area from strong winds and summer rain.*

Graceful Georgian-style windows form the backdrop to an oversized Tasmanian chaise in the formal sitting room. A mahogany-framed convex mirror is complemented by a bust atop a scagiola column.

A TASTE OF THE GOOD LIFE

Sydney columnist, food critic and chief exponent of good living Leo Schofield relishes the finer things of life. When not travelling, writing or sampling the city's latest eateries, he holds court in an elegant two-storey apartment in the diplomatic belt of Sydney's fashionable eastern suburbs. Created from part of a 1920s mansion, the apartment is essentially classic in style, its large rooms forming superb envelopes of space for Mr Schofield's collection of antique furniture, paintings and statues.

A recent renovation opened up several small rooms to create formal living areas, kitchen, bedrooms, bathrooms, gymnasium and wine cellar on the main level, with a new staircase leading to a summer sitting room on the top floor, which in turn opens onto a large paved roof-terrace.

Furniture is an international collection of the best. In the dining room an eighteenth-century Irish table is surrounded by antique English chairs, while an oversized chaise from an old house in Tasmania dominates the formal sitting room.

Mr Schofield's kitchen reflects his professional gourmet status — pots and pans hanging from racks against a background of gleaming stainless steel cupboards, benchtops and appliances, with plates neatly stacked in a fully glassed butler's pantry.

[ABOVE] *Detail of the ornate cast-iron gate post and sandstone fence.*

[LEFT] *The old house peeps through the trees, at the end of a leafy driveway.*

[RIGHT] *A butler's tray provides the only hint of what is behind the end panel in the dining room — a cleverly concealed, mirrored drinks cabinet.*

[FAR RIGHT] *The panelled dining room has been painted a very pale mauve and the floor covered with sisal. An antique Irish table is complemented by eighteenth-century English chairs. The bust atop a pillar is the only piece of art in the room.*

[BELOW] *The new staircase leads from the entry foyer to the rooftop level. A pair of early-nineteenth-century stone figures in the Egyptian manner stand on faux porphyry bases.*

[OPPOSITE PAGE] *The formal sitting room leads directly into a sculpture gallery. Parquetry flooring and pumpkin-coloured walls with white trim have been used throughout this part of the apartment. Details have deliberately been kept simple.*

[ABOVE] *In the galley kitchen the walk-in butler's pantry occupies one wall, the preparation and cooking area the other.*

[RIGHT] *All elements of plating-up are on full display, neatly stacked in the shelves of the glass-fronted butler's pantry.*

[ABOVE] *The Zanussi oven is centred amid gleaming stainless-steel benchtops, cupboards and drawers. The flooring is industrial rubber.*

[LEFT] *A well-lit bench and sink, and utensils all within an arm's reach, are characteristic of a professional setting for a serious cook.*

[RIGHT] *The summer sitting room on the top level. The overscaled sofa is from George Sherlock in London, the eighteenth-century circular table is mahogany, the scrap screen dates from the nineteenth century.*

[BELOW] *An iron pergola and nineteenth-century English terracotta statue against the trellised chimney visually create an outdoor room on the terrace. The teak table in the foreground was designed by Brian Kiernan of Sedia.*

84

[OPPOSITE PAGE] *Two nineteenth-century campaign chairs complement the reconsituted-sandstone paving of the rooftop terrace.*

DESIGN IN VIEW

Dazzling views of Sydney Harbour were not considered important when this Darling Point apartment was built in the 1930s. Although great attention was given to space and detail, small timber doors leading from the living room to the balcony completely blocked out the magnificent vista across Rushcutters Bay to the city. Graciously proportioned rooms were decorated in dark, dingy colours, and the long, narrow corridor added to the gloom of the interior.

It took a professional couple, Margaret Williams and David Pelerman, together with architect Furio Valich, to realize the full potential of the apartment's size and site.

With an eye toward the extraordinary views, Mr Valich replaced the old timber doors with a sweep of steel-framed glazing opening out to the balcony. Looking inward, he gutted the corridor and added a curved glass block wall that now shields the kitchen, bowing it slightly to provide extra room around a breakfast bar. The kitchen itself was reshaped from a tiny existing kitchen, pantry and butler's quarters into a more generous area with plenty of storage and a laundry.

Throughout, the "good bones" of the apartment were highlighted and amplified, including polished timber flooring, decorative cornices and the Art Deco detailing of the fireplace. The curved balcony was finished in tallowwood decking, and the interior painted white over a green base that eliminates glare from the water and the western exposure.

[ABOVE AND LEFT] *Painter Peter Lewis and owner David Pelerman came up with the idea of using a coat of white paint over green paint for the walls to reduce the glare of a straight white finish. Blue trim, a rich timber floor and simple furnishings of white canvas-covered sofas with modern and antique tables create a setting that does not detract from the views.*

[OPPOSITE PAGE] *The curved balcony space overlooking Sydney's Rushcutters Bay was resurfaced with tallowwood decking, and the deck slats repeated thematically in the pergola. A white awning shields the living room glass.*

[ABOVE] *Architect Furio Valich replaced the existing balcony doors with a sweep of steel-framed glazing and geometric steel cut-outs that pick up the Art Deco elements of the original apartment.*

[RIGHT] *Beyond the new glazed doors, the spectacular harbour and the marina of Sydney's Cruising Yacht Club spread out unobscured.*

89

In the dining room, an old French pine table is teamed with bentwood chairs.

[ABOVE] *A small existing kitchen, pantry and butler's quarters were redesigned to become one good-sized, streamlined kitchen with plenty of storage and laundry facilities.*

[RIGHT] *A new glass block wall between the kitchen and the corridor bulges out slightly to yield extra space for the breakfast bar. A load-bearing steel beam above the glass wall is highlighted in chrome yellow.*

91

In the main bedroom a frosted bull's-eye window over the bed provides light with privacy. Japanese tansu *serve as bedside tables.*

MUSEUM QUALITY

The Milsons Point penthouse of architect Harry Seidler and his wife, Penelope, wasn't designed as a family home. What the Seidlers had in mind was a sleek, chic *pied à terre* designed in the Manhattan mould, a place to entertain, and a mini-MOMA to house the couple's ever-increasing collection of outstanding modern art.

The Seidler penthouse is a glass-and-granite eyrie, where flowing curves and countercurves, lustrous grey Sardinian granite and a massive central void, punctuated by a spiral staircase, come together with a sinuous wall of glass to the west. The design capitalizes on sweeping views of Sydney Harbour, with 25 metre decks on both levels of the apartment.

To showcase the Seidlers' art collection, the finishes and fixtures have been kept clear and elegantly pristine. White walls and granite surfaces combine with modern classics, including chairs designed by Marcel Breuer in 1932, and furniture of Seidler's own design, such as the D-shaped dining table in Tamin granite. The art gallery quality of the interior is enhanced by the design of lighting expert Claude Engle, who designed the lighting for I. M. Pei's recent addition to the Louvre, giving the space what Seidler calls a "museum perfection".

From its vantage point overlooking Sydney Harbour the Seidler penthouse captures one of the city's most spectacular sights — the span of the Harbour Bridge. Two 25 metre decks, one on each level of the apartment, curve out sinuously to embrace the bridge, the water and the city lights.

The Seidlers conceived of this apartment as a quasi-gallery to house their ever-growing collection of fine art, including works by Frank Stella (shown here), Roy Lichtenstein and Hilary Mais. One of Engle's special effects for the apartment: the stairway-to-the-stars lighting up the staircase.

Looking down from the upper level through the central void. By night, the western wall of glass embraces the sparkle of harbour lights; at sunset, the blaze over Sydney Harbour creates a spectacular view.

The two-storey apartment encompasses a vast
372 square metres of space. On the lower level,
grey Sardinian granite flooring extends from the
entrance out to the deck. The double-height
void between the two levels is pierced by a
sculptural quarter-turn staircase.

Looking across the central void from the master
bedroom to the upper-level living area, with a
Roy Lichtenstein work on the far wall. All the
chairs in the apartment are a Marcel Breuer
design, created in 1932 and only recently
released by Breuer's widow for manufacture.
For the most part, the remaining furniture
was designed by Harry Seidler, including the
D shaped granite dining table on the
ground level.

A TOUCH OF NEW YORK

Kerry Crowley, director of a Sydney gallery, Yuill Crowley, lives and works on the top floor of an old Surry Hills furniture factory. From the street the wedge-shaped warehouse tells nothing of the spaces within: stark rooms painted white on white displaying a collection of conceptual works by such artists as Robert MacPherson, Imants Tillers, Dick Watkins, Janet Burchill, Rosalie Gascoigne and Peter Tyndall.

On moving in, Kerry Crowley restored the top floor to its original three-room layout. The largest of these became the gallery, with windows on three sides flooding the area with natural light. A second room acts as a stockroom and private viewing area. A partition wall, used for extra hanging space, is in fact the back of an all-in-one kitchen unit. Kerry Crowley's private apartment is divided into two general areas by floating cubes, one enclosing a bathroom and the other screening off the sleeping area.

The unique character of the space is conserved by the use of original factory features. Some, such as a pair of sliding doors, were salvaged from elsewhere in the building. Others, such as the four-tiered storage rack for shoe lasts (in the entrance area) and a pair of industrialist machinist's chairs (placed under Robert MacPherson's *Diagram for its Own Hanging*), came from factory sites farther afield.

[RIGHT] *The understated exterior of Kerry Crowley's Surry Hills warehouse.*

[BELOW] *Here in the main living area, original chairs from the 1950s are grouped around a plaid linen rug. On a table behind the sofa rests Joan Grounds's* Ceramic Teapot in Parcel *and an assemblage by Rosalie Gascoigne.*

Well-placed furniture and objects are enhanced
by the stream of natural light that floods
the space.

[RIGHT] *A four-tiered storage rack for shoe lasts and an original sliding door accentuate the unique character of the space. A Gunter Christmann painting hangs on the wall.*

[BELOW, LEFT] *A sculpture by Gay Hawkes is juxtaposed against the clean lines of Robert MacPherson's corner painting.*

[BELOW, RIGHT] *Kerry Crowley polished the floors, unblocked windows and painted all walls white on white to create light and spacious living areas. In the foreground stands a Kafka-designed armchair from the 1950s.*

[ABOVE] *On a table top, casually arranged flowers are teamed with a carefully considered grouping of objects.*

[LEFT] *The view from the northwest corner of the apartment, which is drenched in morning sunlight.*

[ABOVE] *Imants Tillers'* St Francis Taking the Rosary *dominates the sleeping area. The bed is covered with a hand-embroidered quilt which dates back to the 1920s.*

[ABOVE, LEFT] *In the bedroom, Rosalie Gascoigne's assemblage of thistles in chipped enamel utensils behind a glass windscreen.*

[OPPOSITE PAGE] *Janet Burchill's* Equivalence *hangs in the bedroom. The cupboard on the left was made during the Depression era.*

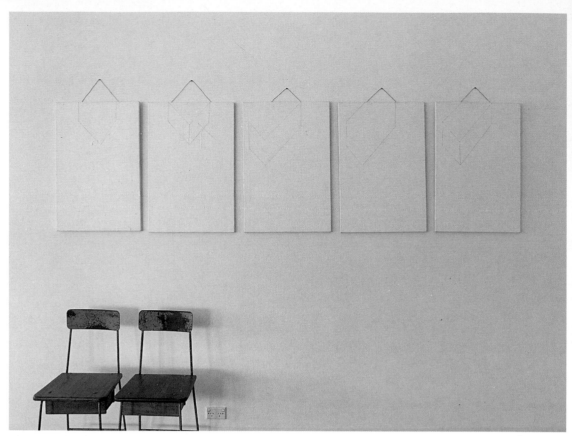

[ABOVE] *In the kitchen, adjacent to the main living area, a massive old factory table seats fourteen comfortably. The back of the floating wall to the galley kitchen acts as hanging space in the private viewing area.*

[ABOVE, RIGHT] *A pair of industrial machinist's chairs beneath Robert MacPherson's* Diagram for its Own Hanging.

[RIGHT] *The uncluttered lines of the Yuill Crowley Gallery.*

[LEFT] *A floating cube in the apartment encloses the bathroom.*

[BELOW] *The clean white surfaces of the bathroom are contrasted with Janet Burchill's* Temptation to Exist.

H O U S E S

Beyond the terrace-fringed streets of the inner-city areas, the wider swathe of harbourside, bayside and garden suburbs in Australia embraces an eclectic assortment of houses and design sensibilities.

Where a well-defined style of period architecture exists, the conventional wisdom is to follow it through with a sympathetic interior treatment. That sympathetic treatment need not be a faithful gallop alongside the architecture with period furniture — Victorian tables in Victorian dining rooms — but rather a well-struck chord of agreement, such as Appley Hoare's Federation-meets-farmhouse approach to her turn-of-the-century house on Sydney's North Shore.

Renovation of an old house can also follow new paths away from the follies of the existing building, as demonstrated by Espie Dods's elegant Mediterranean reinterpretation of an old four-room cottage for John and Caroline Laws, where a broken-down workhorse of a building has been transformed into a Tuscan villa complete with loggia — and looks completely at home in its surroundings.

The choice of an architect is a creative act in itself: the clients who chose Nicholas Bochsler revealed their desire for a bold design of sweep and scale and a dynamic departure from the traditional gravity-bound enclosed Australian house. Unfettered by direct historical references, the interior design has found new points of reference to respond to — refreshing and expanding the vocabulary of Australian style.

[LEFT] *This Federation-style house has been clothed in a wardrobe of vibrantly coloured architectural trims.*

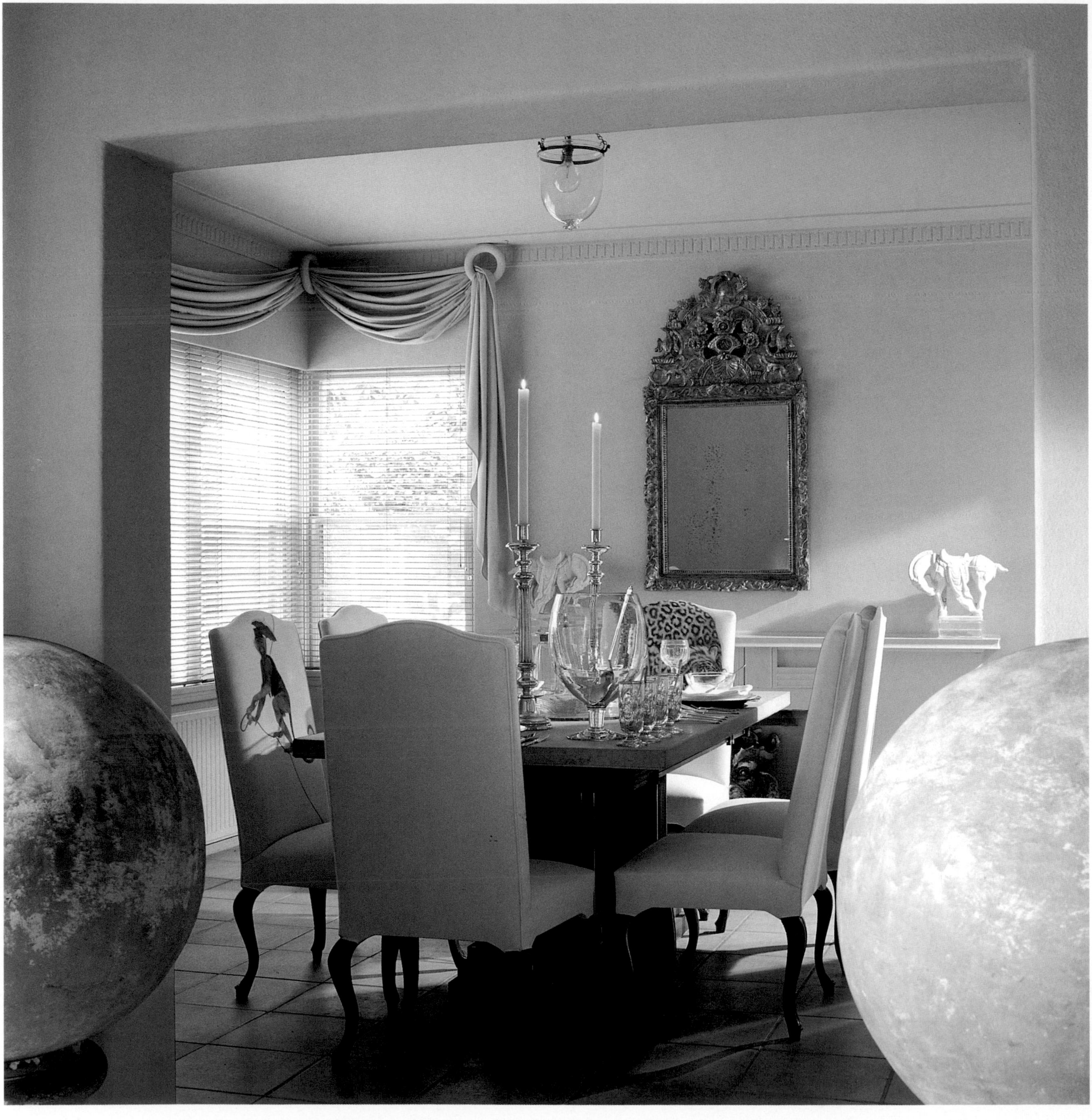

CHIC ECLECTICISM

From the street Georgina Weir's Art Deco-style house looks like many of its neighbours. Elegantly fashioned wrought-iron gates and sweeping driveways are typical of Toorak, Melbourne, as are manicured gardens set amid large trees.

The interior of the house is at once austere and flamboyant. Materials usually associated with outdoors, such as concrete and stone, are mixed with European antiques, Art Deco furnishings and circus artwork. Huge glass vases, massed with flowers, stand on a concrete slab floor, alongside equally huge stone balls from the Kensington Horse Barracks in London. The floor is a story in itself. Ordinary unsealed-concrete garden slabs were simply laid on top of the existing floor. Without finish of any kind, they are simply washed when necessary.

The house is filled with deft flashes of the unexpected. Dining chairs are individually handpainted, while sofas and chairs are covered in lengths of 1930s tie fabrics found in a warehouse and painstakingly stitched together. Painted tin angels hold the specially made drape rings, and an ornate upright giraffe grand piano sits waiting to be played.

[ABOVE] *The entrance hall, with arum lilies massed in a huge vase and a statue carved from stone, sets the scene for the rest of the house as a successful mix of the flamboyant and the austere.*

[LEFT] *Crafted wrought-iron gates and a sweeping driveway lead to the house.*

[OPPOSITE PAGE] *The elegant dining room features handpainted chairs, each with a different design. The huge stone balls in the foreground came from the Kensington Horse Barracks, London.*

[ABOVE] *Simple concrete slabs were used to tile the floors in many rooms.*

[RIGHT] *French cast-lead garden dogs bracket the fireplace. The drinks stand on the Louis-style sofa is a Japanese scribe's table.*

*The music room, with its upright giraffe piano. On the wall is a panel
from a seventeenth-century French wallpaper.*

[LEFT] *The handpainted dining chairs are decorated with circus motifs.*

[FAR LEFT] *Above the fireplace hangs an etched mirror from the 1930s luxury passenger ship* Normandie.

[BELOW, LEFT] *The family pet catnaps on fake ocelot draped over a sofa.*

[BELOW, FAR LEFT] *A painted tin angel holds a drape in the music room.*

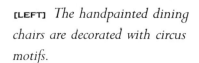

[RIGHT AND FAR RIGHT] *The simplicity of line and colour extends through to the kitchen, where the benchtops are concrete.*

[BELOW] *Chairs and sofas are upholstered in 1930s tie fabrics, and coir matting covers the floor. Artichokes, leeks and asparagus make an unusual table decoration.*

[OPPOSITE PAGE] *The wrought-iron door opening onto the courtyard was created by Don Browne for the owner.*

112

COMFORTABLE FORMALITY

A Palladian-inspired villa, tucked behind a creamy-apricot wall in Woollahra, is the Sydney home of Australia's best-known and the world's most highly paid radio star, John Laws, and his wife, Caroline.

From the simple street door set in a high wall, through the formal front *parterre*, and up the wide flight of steps to the loggia, the strong Mediterranean influence continues through the house and beyond, to the elegant swimming pool set against a high brick wall which is panelled with mirrors to give an illusionary reflection of distance.

Dating from 1840, the original house was a four-roomed cottage made from sandstone and rubble, with a central hallway and a kitchen at the back. Architect Espie Dods rebuilt the whole house, opening out the poky little rooms on the ground floor to create free-flowing living areas.

The garden is Mrs Laws's special love, and here she combines architectural formality with lush, perfumed greenery. A background of clipped and disciplined hedges, dramatized by urns and pots, evokes the grand gardens of Italy and France, although wistaria and honeysuckle, tumbling over each other in wild abandon, soften the edges of walls and pergolas. Two varieties of Virginia creeper entwine to engulf the house, their tendrils scrambling up the columns of the loggia and across the ceiling to droop gently earthwards, where they meet the smooth glass of the central skylight.

[ABOVE] *A marble nude gazes contemplatively into the reflective swimming pool. The pool is set in sandstone and enclosed at the far end by a mirrored brick wall.*

[RIGHT] *The marble-floored loggia is furnished with cane chairs and small tables made from antique Thai drums. A circular skylight provides a frame for tendrils of Virginia creeper. Beyond is the formal* parterre *garden.*

[ABOVE] *A view of the house from the garden shows a contrast of the formality of clipped box hedges and rampant, unmanicured vines. Massed sloping beds of white roses stand out against the surrounding deep greens, visually underscoring the approach to the wide loggia.*

[LEFT] *Seated on a globe and holding grapes and a wine glass, this stone cherub is one of a pair of eighteenth-century putti in the loggia.*

In the red drawing room the Laws's collection includes Japanese paintings from a set of seventeenth-century sliding doors, a late eighteenth-century walnut commode, and, on the Japanese lacquered coffee table, a Rodin sculpture.

[LEFT] *A double inside-out play of perspectives was created in the red sitting room, with a mirrored wall casting back a reflection of the interior while flanking gunslot windows draw the eye outward to columns outside. The modern marble head is a sculpture by Joel Allenburg of his wife, Anna.*

[BELOW, LEFT] *Artefacts arrayed on the walnut commode include a fifteenth-century Korean pot and an ancient Persian spearhead, believed to date from about 14 000 BC.*

[BELOW, RIGHT] *Rose,* by Auguste Rodin, *was the artist's wife. She married him when quite young, survived many mistresses and was with him when he died.*

[THIS PAGE AND OPPOSITE] *In John Laws's study the mood is dark and contemplative: finished in a library green, it is walled with books and complete with a collection of fountain pens and paper knives. The desk is a late seventeenth-century Spanish piece. The bird on the desk dates from pre-Columbian Mexico, and the small pottery jar filled with flowers dates back to the Neolithic period, its ring base from the early Bronze Age. On one side table stands a serene eighteenth-century Buddha; nearby, a seventeenth-century Japanese red lacquer bowl.*

FORTRESS IN WATER AND GLASS

A black ceramic-tiled exterior presents a solid facade to the streetscape in Toorak, Melbourne, giving no hint of the light, spacious world behind its walls. Architects Bochsler and Partners designed this house around two intangible elements—reflection and light—and then went on to frame them, link them, exploit them, creating shapes, voids, vistas, moving shadows and shimmering surfaces.

The generous use of space, the tall white walls and the sweep of polished black granite flooring come together to create a powerful visual dynamic. The shimmering pool is positioned so that guests in the dining room look out through a glass wall to a water garden, punctuated with rocks and a path of stepping stones.

There is a constant change in levels. Floors go up or down one step at a time. In some places the ceilings match their path; in others they contradict it. Light moves constantly across and around the building, creating patches of brilliant sunlight and areas of cool shadow. Pools shimmer everywhere. A swimming pool sits suspended between two walls of glass, while another, purely for visual delight, looks like a piece of glass, so still is its surface.

[RIGHT] *A path of black granite stepping stones punctuates the water garden.*

[BELOW] *The design of the house plays on reflection and light. Frameless glass forms a transparent surround on the balcony, and a mirror-still pool reflects the objects around it.*

[LEFT] *Inside and out, lines and planes are reflected in shimmering water.*

[FAR LEFT] *A steel trellis erected across the roof bears a cluster of flowering climbers.*

[BELOW] *Bochsler's design generates a dynamic interplay of angle against angle.*

121

[RIGHT] *Once again, the reflective qualities of glass and water are explored, with a swimming pool bounded by walls of glass.*

[FAR RIGHT] *Tall white walls and a sweep of polished black granite flooring reinforce the cool, majestic language of the architecture.*

[RIGHT] *The house creates spaces, and plays with the links between them.*

[OPPOSITE PAGE] *Black granite flooring meets white granite in the family area of the house.*

FOLLOWING IN THE MASTER'S FOOTSTEPS

American architect Walter Burley Griffin, who designed Australia's national capital, Canberra, bought the bushy promontory of Castlecrag overlooking Sydney's Middle Harbour in 1920 and then set about designing a group of houses which were to blend with the environment. Roads meandered around the contours of the land, skirting rock outcrops and native trees. The original fifteen sandstone houses designed for the peninsula were rugged in appearance, with flat roofs so that everyone could enjoy the views.

Seventy years later this house by architect Alex Popov won the 1990 Robin Boyd Award, the highest national architectural prize for residential work, and was described by the judges as a "reverent tribute to Griffin . . . but a beautiful and liveable building, which responded to the needs of the client and the constraints of the site". While the design broadly follows the Burley Griffin philosophy, it differs dramatically in that it is light and free-flowing, whereas the American's were boxy and dark.

Popov's use of planes recalls the advice of Frank Lloyd Wright: "If you see a hill, never touch the top of it; put an eyebrow on it. In building in terraces, remember the stepping effect, the planes."

[ABOVE] *Neighbours' views are preserved by the house's flat roofline, while skylights draw in the northern light.*

[LEFT] *Like the Burley Griffin houses of the 1920s, Popov's design blends with the Castlecrag environment.*

[FAR LEFT] *Large windows allow views of Sydney's Middle Harbour.*

[RIGHT] *Natural light is drawn into the kitchen from the skylight.*

[BELOW] *The inner sanctum: an open-sided, columned dining room. Materials used for the floor progress from marble to sandstone to ash.*

127

[LEFT] "... a beautiful and liveable building, which responded to the needs of the client and the constraints of the site."

FEDERATION FLAVOUR

Antique dealer and interior designer Appley Hoare discovered this large Federation house while advising a developer-friend in a professional capacity. Situated in the Sydney harbourside suburb of Neutral Bay, it had been converted over several decades into fourteen cheaply rented flats. Yet the views of the harbour and distant city were spectacular, the staircase indeed grand, and somehow the lofty ceilings, delicate plasterwork and detailed joinery had survived the butchery of earlier renovations.

With panoramas from every window, Ms Hoare opted for a simple, uncluttered interior: all-white walls, ceilings and woodwork. With the dark varnished staircase and downstairs floors stripped and polished, she carefully placed favourite country-style pieces in position: an early Australian table, an English pine chest, nostalgic cane on the verandah, a French wine cage in the kitchen and, for contrast, a sleek Italian grey leather sofa and chairs in the sitting room. Accessories include early pine-framed mirrors, a miniature dresser, an antique pine trough, a wooden sheep and assorted forms of the letter "A", for Appley.

[ABOVE, LEFT] *A stark white passageway leads to the small curved verandah, an ideal spot for drinks or an alfresco lunch.*

[ABOVE, RIGHT] *An old pine mirror complements the simple elegance of a traditional marble mantel.*

[LEFT] *Stunning views are highlighted by the intricate woodwork and the colours of the Federation-style verandah.*

City and harbour views from the bay window make a perfect backdrop to the all-white upstairs living room.

An Australian pine farm table and early
Australian beech chairs form the nucleus of a
country dining room in a suburban house.

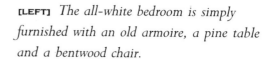

[LEFT] *The all-white bedroom is simply furnished with an old armoire, a pine table and a bentwood chair.*

[FAR LEFT] *A pewter and porcelain warming carvery dish rests on the dining table. In the window bay is an English Baltic pine chest c. 1800, with giant tin measure and antique farm trough.*

131

The original staircase was stripped to match the polished floorboards. The English pine chest and the floral display continue the country theme of the house.

This handsome iron campaign couch
was manufactured in Gawler, South Australia,
and dates from the 1860s. The Australian
naive paintings are typical of work done in the
nineteenth century.

COLLECTOR'S CORNER

An attraction to Australian colonial furniture as a budget-conscious student in the early 1970s has led to a grand passion and a successful antique business for Adelaide migrant Y. Khai Liew. Grappling with the figures and theories associated with an economics course, Mr Liew became bored, preferring to fossick around in second-hand furniture shops. Three years after his arrival he opened his first antique shop, specializing in Australian furniture and folk art.

Never too interested in formal Anglo-Irish pieces, he preferred the local, rustic items from the Barossa Valley and surrounding hill towns. This area of South Australia was settled in the 1840s by sects of Lutherans fleeing from religious persecution in their native Germany. Hardworking country folk, determined to make good in their new homeland, they set about doing what they could do best, planting grapes for wine. Along with their winemaking expertise they brought building and cabinet-making skills, which, for the most part, went unrecognized outside their own community.

Mr Liew finds the country pieces surprisingly artistic for their simplicity. "They are particularly appropriate for Adelaide, which for me still possesses a certain provincial charm, agrarian pace and texture, which is soft and welcoming," he says.

[ABOVE] *A mid-nineteenth-century food cupboard from the Barossa Valley, with its original red-painted finish, flanked by a pair of rare casuarina chairs, c. 1870. The naive oil paintings date from the end of the nineteenth century and are also South Australian.*

[LEFT] *This pine Biedermeier-style dresser dates from the 1860s. At either side, Hepplewhite-style chairs produced fifty years earlier and cedar and pine chessboards from the late nineteenth century were all made in South Australia.*

[RIGHT] *A nineteenth-century carved redgum duck decoy rests atop a painted pine Germanic cupboard, c. 1860.*

[BELOW] *On top of a blanket chest a German-style mixing bowl holds painted redgum bowling balls (detail far right). The naive paintings, carvings and miniature dressing table were common decorative items in nineteenth-century South Australian households.*

[LEFT] *A typical South Australian household scene from the nineteenth century: two pine chairs, c. 1870, stand either side of a redgum table, with a redgum bench in the foreground. The carved decoy, painted cutlery tray and pottery jug are complemented by two naive paintings by H.W. Green and an oil portrait of an early settler.*

[BELOW] *Two early South Australian Germanic pieces: a Biedermeier-style couch in red gum and pine, c. 1860, and, in the foreground, a late nineteenth-century washstand base in pine and metal. The nineteenth-century metal portrait plaque is European in origin; the pair of mid-nineteenth-century frames are made from rare Australian muskwood.*

NO AUSTRALIAN CITY IS TOO FAR from a slice of country, and no Australian city dweller is ever too far from a weekend haven of beach or bush — or both. For Sydneysiders, the Pittwater area is only an hour away from the city centre, yet it is as scenically remote as the wildest, farthest shore, with holiday homes perched on gum-clad bluffs that plunge steeply to the water. Style here is common sense: easy-care salt-resistant-surfaces, a minimum of clutter in minimal spaces, and a relaxed sense of place. An old boathouse, revived with cheerful paintwork and physically extended with a wrap-around deck, incorporates all the best of a Pittwater retreat, inside and out.

On the Queensland coast, architect Daryl Jackson created a beach house of a more formal design, yet endowed it with the easy grace and hideaway atmosphere of simpler beach cottages. Down south, on the Mornington Peninsula, where clients required a retreat of luxurious proportions, Melbourne architect Ermin Smrekar responded with a design that reflects that brief, without sacrificing a relaxed holiday feeling.

Glenn Murcutt's celebrated design for a house in Moruya takes the beach and bush theme to its logical extreme — a house that takes its cue from a tent and shields itself from the sun while soaking in the views.

[LEFT] *Magnificent bush and water views over Port Phillip Bay are one of the attractions of Melbourne's Mornington Peninsula.*

RADICAL TENT

If there can be such a thing as "pure" modern Australian architecture, the claim could be made for Glenn Murcutt's artful corrugated-iron and concrete-slab houses, brilliant imagings of the Australian way of life, executed in basic industrial materials.

Mr Murcutt's work has been referred to as "radical shed chic". For this beach house in Moruya, he has engineered a radical tent for clients who had gone camping on this site for many years. Like a tent, the house represents the debunking of the front door while it celebrates the freedom of a barefoot existence.

The distinctive winged roofline takes its cue from the sloping site. Rainwater is collected in the cleft of the wings and channelled into an underground tank. Response to the sun and the changing seasons was an integral part of the design. The steel frame was reverse-brick-veneered, with the internal veneer providing a thermal "sink". Northern overhangs deflect the high summer sun but allow deep penetration of sunlight in winter.

This is a house with an overcoat, says Mr Murcutt, for the south side is well protected from southerly winds from the snowfields. Windows have been kept minimal here, while the sheltered northern and eastern walls are fully glazed.

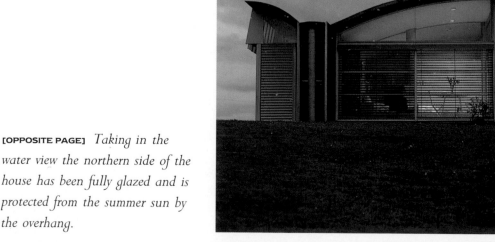

[ABOVE] *Retractable exterior blinds on the northern and eastern sides of the house are used to cope with changing seasons and climatic conditions.*

[RIGHT] *The main bedroom occupies the prime location on the northeastern corner of the house.*

[OPPOSITE PAGE] *Taking in the water view the northern side of the house has been fully glazed and is protected from the summer sun by the overhang.*

Detail of the roofline on the western side. The cleft between the roof wings is a rainwater collector. A lunette window provides a circular element to the arcs of the design.

140

[RIGHT] *The house was built on the brow of the hillside site with an east–west axis, "from the centre of Australia to the Pacific Ocean", says the architect. The opening to the left of the northern facade is a small courtyard between the parents' wing to the east and the children's and guests' wing to the west. Both wings are completely self-contained.*

[LEFT] *The two roof wings allude to the contours of the sloping site. The front wing returns slightly to earth, while the arc of the upslope wing does not fall below the vertical.*

[FAR LEFT] *A close-up view of the closed external Ventral blinds. Overhead, the curved arc of the roof and its supporting struts resemble the tent form that was the inspiration for this house.*

[OPPOSITE PAGE] *The rainwater transport system on the cleft roofline echoes the "people transport" corridor system beneath the cleft inside.*

[LEFT] *The parents' wing has its own entrance.*

[BELOW, LEFT] *A small courtyard connects the living and kitchen area of the parents' wing with the children's and guests' living/kitchen area. Sliding doors allow the two separate areas to be opened up as one large entertaining space.*

[BELOW, CENTRE] *Living and bedroom areas are located on the glazed northern side of the house. On the south side of the corridor spine are the kitchen, bathroom and laundry facilities.*

143

[BELOW, RIGHT] *Views from the parents' bedroom take in land and waterscapes. Sliding glass doors are sun-shielded by external louvre blinds.*

BACK TO BASICS

A one-room hut with a dirt floor and bark-lined corrugated-iron roof is hardly the typical weekender for a young film director, but it is her way of getting back to her Australian heritage. Set in a bush clearing in central western New South Wales and surrounded by tall eucalypts and flowering sago bush, the hut is similar to the rough dwellings built by early pioneers. Young saplings were used as framing for walls and to support the central pitched roof and wide verandah. Unmatched second-hand windows and doors collected locally and furniture picked up at clearing sales or film sets give the place a haphazard kind of outback style.

Inside, improvization is the name of the game: homemade chairs, a table rescued from a miner's hut, an old sofa covered with a bedspread, and a collection of practical *objets* and tin cooking utensils.

Shelves and benchtops are split logs cut to size, and plates and utensils sit in slatted shelves made from odd pieces of timber. Worn rugs and carpet squares cover the packed dirt floor, with a lopsided mantelpiece made from yet more saplings and a couple of old planks.

There is no electricity, but kerosene lamps provide adequate light, supplemented by two romantic candles attached to the back of the old cast-iron bedstead. Water comes from an outside tank, and a solid-fuel stove takes care of cooking requirements.

[RIGHT] *The view towards the dam and the distant hills.*

[BELOW] *The slab hut sits in a small clearing surrounded by tall eucalypts. Young treetrunks were used for the verandah posts.*

[OPPOSITE PAGE] *An old table from a shearers' hut, a bench and odd chairs furnish the eating area. The pole in the foreground supports the steeply pitched roof.*

146

[RIGHT] *The living area. The firehood is made from a shaped piece of metal, which has been set behind a rough timber mantelpiece.*

[BELOW, LEFT TO RIGHT] *The kitchen worktable. Cast-iron cooking utensils hang above the small solid-fuel stove, which provides extra heating during winter. The bench and sink surround is split timber, and open shelves display china, enamelware and saucepans.*

[ABOVE AND LEFT] *The bedroom area is dominated by a pitched roof lined with bark between exposed branch beams. Old rugs and carpet pieces cover the dirt floor. Note the holders for candles on each side of the iron bedstead. At night the dwelling is romantically lit by candles, kerosene lamps and the glow of the fire.*

[ABOVE, LEFT] *The corrugated iron bathroom, with its variety of windows. Water for the enamelled cast-iron bath is warmed by a chip heater.*

[ABOVE, RIGHT] *The traditional loo.*

[RIGHT] *For guests who prefer to shower, a waterbag with nozzle is strung above the bath.*

[BELOW] *A gypsy caravan makes an unconventional guest room.*

148

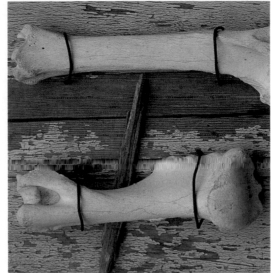

[TOP LEFT TO BOTTOM RIGHT] *An old yellow chair with sliced log seat, legs made of tree boughs, and a roughly shaped back rail; bone handles for a simple door fastening; a more-traditional door handle, aged with time; an old bush table on the verandah, which has been roughly paved with stone from the property; an elegant chair frame given new life with tongue-and-groove timber; and a chest of drawers made from kerosene tins—not original, but recreated for a film set.*

IN ITS ELEMENT

Daryl Jackson's design for a Mission Beach holiday house takes its cue from the traditional Australian beach house, and then goes on to proclaim the architectural aesthetic of its own time in a simple but immensely eloquent way. The wide-roofed verandahs, louvred windows and shiplap-board interiors of beach houses along the length of the Australian coast have been reworked by the Melbourne-based architect to create a home of intelligent simplicity.

The house is essentially a free flow of space, but the architect has worked to ensure the privacy of guests by creating a number of independent spaces. Living areas on the main floor are defined by the arrangement of well-worn armchairs and framed by telegraph poles, sanded to a smooth finish. The covered stairway leads down to a second bedroom and bathroom for guests. The structure turns in on itself at one end, protecting the house from a nearby road and forming a secluded courtyard.

Air flow was crucial to the design of the house — given the often oppressive humidity of the Queensland climate. Jackson made use of a number of traditional features to ensure a constant flow of air in and around the house: the house-on-stilts structure allows air to circulate below the floorboards, while a row of ceiling-high folding glass doors opens onto a wide verandah, capitalizing on sea breezes drifting in from the east.

[ABOVE] *A path leads from the garden onto the beach.*

[CENTRE] *Jackson's design echoes the traditional structure of Queensland coastal houses.*

[RIGHT] *Mission Beach is part of Queensland's "island coast". Dunk Island and Bedarra lie within sight of the beach.*

[OPPOSITE PAGE] *The beach house is, above all, comfortable. The owners have chosen to furnish their home simply and practically. The natural materials used for the interior, including polished brushbox floorboards and old telegraph poles, evoke a sense of calm.*

[ABOVE] *Jackson's design offsets the oppressive humidity of the Queensland climate by ensuring a constant flow of air in and around the house. Folding glass doors open up the house to cool coastal breezes drifting in from the east.*

[RIGHT] *The house is built on stilts, allowing air to circulate underneath.*

153

[ABOVE] *Steamer chairs on the wide verandah offer views of Mission Beach and Dunk Island beyond.*

[LEFT] *Jackson has used telegraph poles throughout the house. This one makes an attractive but unusual garden bench.*

[FAR LEFT] *The owners have encouraged the growth of tropical vegetation to shield the house from the public eye. But the native garden yields more than privacy.*

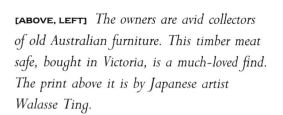

[ABOVE, LEFT] *The owners are avid collectors of old Australian furniture. This timber meat safe, bought in Victoria, is a much-loved find. The print above it is by Japanese artist Walasse Ting.*

[ABOVE, RIGHT] *This striking tropical foliage was collected at the beach's edge.*

[RIGHT] *The tranquillity of the room, created by weathered timber and white walls, is broken by a colourful Mexican quilt on the far wall and a painting by Aboriginal artist Paddy Nbitjana in the bedroom beyond.*

Sanded telegraph poles have an important
structural function, forming the stilts that set
the house above ground level. They also ensure
the security of the roof in an area subject to
tropical cyclones.

[RIGHT] *A view of the dining area from the verandah.*

[BELOW, LEFT] *The owners reap the benefit of encouraging a native garden. A work by Aboriginal artist Isabel Namanijira hangs on the wall behind.*

[BELOW CENTRE] *A basket of fruit adds a casual flash of colour.*

[BELOW, RIGHT] *Jackson's telegraph poles frame a sleek, modern kitchen.*

156

[ABOVE, LEFT] *A covered stairway leads down to additional sleeping quarters and an extra bathroom.*

[ABOVE, RIGHT] *The exterior of the house is reminiscent of the traditional architecture of the Queensland coast.*

[LEFT] *The house turns in on itself to create a secluded courtyard.*

SEASIDE MODERN

The small town of Sorrento overlooking Port Phillip Bay was the site of the first white settlement in Victoria. By the latter half of the nineteenth century, the cliffs of Sorrento were well populated. Houses were made of limestone and could only be reached by paddlesteamer and horse and cart.

All this is a far cry from one dramatically modern residence there today. Designed by architect Ermin Smrekar, it is a house of light and free-flowing space. For the exterior, the architect used a lagoon-green sympathetic to the bush and bayside site; inside, a uniform wash of colour, created by white walls and polished stone floors, allows the splendour of the natural surroundings to dominate the house. Glazed walls embrace magnificent ocean views.

The land is sloping, falling away on several sides, but the architect was determined to make a feature of the irregularity. "We had two choices: either we could bulldoze the whole area, which is something I have never done, or we could work with the site and add interest to the house." Smrekar's design incorporates the natural fall of the land, with five internal levels stepping down to the edge of the property.

The grounds of the house are immaculate, the retaining walls set flush with lush green lawns. A semi-circular spa pool sits on the edge of the cliff. Conceived as a "horizon pool", its lines flow away from the eye and seem to merge with the ocean beyond.

[TOP] *Complex geometries, stepped levels and extensive glazing are important features of the design, visually breaking up the physical mass of a large house.*

[CENTRE] *Smrekar used multiple levels, inside and out, to accommodate the natural slope of the land.*

[LEFT] *The spa is designed so that the outermost border drops away. From the house, the pool seems to merge with the ocean beyond.*

Once part of the original property, the timber jetty and boatshed have been restored by the present owners.

[ABOVE] *Smrekar has allowed the natural beauty of Port Phillip Bay to dominate the grounds of the house. A flawless lawn and immaculate entertaining areas keep distractions to a minimum.*

[RIGHT] *White walls and polished stone floors help to make the interior of the house a continuous free-flowing space. The stone, imported from Yugoslavia, was chosen for uniformity of colour and pattern.*

[ABOVE] *Smrekar chose a pale lagoon-green for the exterior of the house, a colour that complements the blue-green tones of bush and ocean.*

[RIGHT] *The secluded position of the house allows the owners the luxury of this extravagant glass entranceway.*

161

BOATSHED REFUGE

With its feet literally standing in water, this old boatshed has survived almost a century of tides, winds, baking sun and driving rain. Built where Ku-ring-gai Chase National Park meets the shores of Sydney's Pittwater, it provides a weekend retreat for architect Sophie Wilson and her family. Here they fish, swim, walk through the surrounding bush, or just sit listening to the gentle sound of water lapping under the floorboards.

Accessible only by water, the boatshed dates back to 1912, when it was built as a storage shed for a large estate. Now restored and painted white with a mauve-blue trim, the little building stands sentinel-like overlooking a wide sandy bay.

The place is so small that great discipline is required to avoid clutter. Only items constantly used and loved are allowed: practical pine and wicker furniture; hatstands in lieu of bulky wardrobes; shelves for books and shell collections; racks for fishing rods. Model ships and cars are housed on the ceiling crossbeams, and marine pictures grouped together on the limited wall space.

The boatshed seen against a gum-studded Pittwater bluff. Originally a storage shed for a large estate, the little boatshed was built in 1912, and is accessible only by water.

[ABOVE] *The new owners replaced paintwork corroded by time and salt with a fresh, cheerful finish of white with wistaria and pale blue trim.*

[LEFT] *A flow-through inside-outside feeling from the living space to the deck is reinforced by the floorboards butting up to the decking timber.*

[ABOVE] *The original roof tiles were laid flat on the diagonal, an unusual treatment for Sydney. French doors on two sides of the boatshed provide a feeling of intimate contact with the surrounding waterscape.*

[RIGHT AND FAR RIGHT] *The living area is located to the right, with bedrooms off to one side of the shed. Hatstands are used in lieu of wardrobes to conserve space.*

A well-weathered lifebuoy, a dinghy and a chair painted with a mermaid are in keeping with the salt-spray atmosphere of the boatshed's setting.

[CENTRE, LEFT TO RIGHT] *The sizeable deck around the boatshed provides plenty of outdoor area for lazing about in the sun and taking in the salt air. At night, the sound of the water lapping at the piers below creates a sense of being aboard a yacht.*

[BOTTOM, LEFT TO RIGHT] *Keeping it simple: collections of shells, marine artwork and colourful fishing rods provide decorative touches appropriate to a get-away-from-it-all boatshed retreat.*

THE NOTION OF "COUNTRY LIVING" evokes images of grand rural living and the prosperity of the halcyon days, when Australia rode on the sheep's back and a modest property included more land than a horse could cover in three days.

But country living embraces different meanings, different styles. Retreating from the pace of urban living, some Australians have established stylish redoubts just beyond the city limits. Designer and artist Jenny Kee has taken up residence in a superb mountain studio-house created by architect Glenn Murcutt, while architect Guilford Bell has reinterpreted the traditional Australian bush house as a sculptural white design for Melbourne clients who wanted to live away from it all on the Mornington Peninsula. Further afield, an old mill has been converted into a home for an Adelaide businessman. And in Victoria's Macedon Ranges a brand-new country house has been designed with a built-in patina of age.

Grander, but by no means large country properties such as Rosebank in South Australia give another meaning to country living. Finally there are the huge isolated homesteads such as Woolmers, with its grand rosewood and mahogany appointments, and a complete village of outbuildings.

[LEFT] *This Queensland stands in splendid isolation amid lush rainforest.*

167

[THIS PAGE AND OPPOSITE] *Alongside an existing old house, architect Glenn Murcutt created a pair of bush pavilions in the Blue Mountains. One wing is a living area, the other a gallery. Architectural details are reminiscent of the integrity of traditional structures such as the sturdy gates of Australia's farmlands. Between the pavilions are pieces from Kenny Kee's collection of contemporary Aboriginal carvings.*

IN KEY WITH THE BUSH

Such is fashion and fabric designer Jenny Kee's affinity with the Australian land that many of her designs are inspired by the Dreamtime stories of the first inhabitants. The house she shares with artist Michael Ramsden in the Blue Mountains of New South Wales is an extension of her extroversion and sense of colour and design, tempered by his more meditative and contemplative approach to life.

Beside a turn-of-the-century timber house set in a bush clearing, architect Glenn Murcutt has designed two pavilion-like structures in redwood and corrugated iron. One comprises a living area, the second a gallery, with a glass wall overlooking a courtyard paved in blue metal stone. The materials used are those of the early white settlers, the ambience created a modern adaptation of a primitive world.

The exterior is painted silvery-grey, reflecting the bark from surrounding trees. Interiors are a combination of stark white walls and natural timber floors, the perfect backdrop to Michael Ramsden's paintings and the eclectic display of furniture and artefacts. These are signature Jenny Kee—strong, dramatic and colourful. Many are her own adaptations of Aboriginal designs, symbolic of the Dreamtime; others, by Gay Hawkes and Roland Clarke, are illustrative of the sophisticated use of recycled bush materials such as corrugated iron, eucalypt twigs and packing-case timbers.

[RIGHT AND OPPOSITE PAGE] *In the living area, contemporary Aboriginal carvings, Michael Ramsden's paintings and weaves designed by Jenny Kee come together naturally in a harmonious relationship born of a mutual affinity with the Australian land.*

[BELOW] *Ceramic bowl by Michael Ramsden and Graham Oldroyd.*

[LEFT] *Detail of a Jenny Kee rug, with old carved stools by Roland Clarke.*

[RIGHT] *The kitchen, at one end of the open-plan living area.*

[ABOVE AND LEFT] *The bathroom features walls of Quilpie rock opal and ceramic murals of an Aboriginal legend by Michael Ramsden and Graham Oldroyd. The old-fashioned bathtub has been teamed with an ultra-modern shower capsule. Timeless objects — rocks and shells — line two ceramic bowls.*

[ABOVE, LEFT TO RIGHT] *Beads and ceramic bowl on display in the gallery; modern bush chair with a fanback of timber oddments and rough blue-edged treetrunk table with twig pedestal by Roland Clarke; modern bush chair with a rough slatted timber back and axe-like top crossbar by Gay Hawkes.*

[RIGHT] *The glazed walls of the gallery reveal a backdrop of eucalyptus trees native to the area and fine specimens of conifers.*

[OPPOSITE PAGE] *A tree figure made of eucalypt twigs by Danton Hughes and a corrugated-iron tub chair by Roland Clarke bracket the woodpile on the verandah.*

HIGH-STYLE HOMESTEAD

Less than a decade ago this patch of land in Officer, in the Victorian countryside, was an apple orchard. Today it is the site of a spectacularly innovative example of modern Australian architecture. Architect Guilford Bell has used the traditional structures and materials of an Australian country house to create a dramatic, but practical residence for the owners of a Melbourne plant nursery, The City Garden.

The exterior of the house features materials common to most Australian country houses. Corrugated iron has been used not only for the tall, curved roof but also for the exterior walls. The area around the house is paved with second-hand bricks salvaged from the old Glen Iris brickworks and is shaded by timber screens.

Inside, spaces are carved out of the simplest of geometries, a square, with three bedrooms and a kitchen in the four corners. Living and dining areas occupy the remaining open space, defined by timber screens and squares of carpeting. The simplicity of white walls, white carpets and white upholstered furniture focuses attention on the magnificent grounds, created jointly by Bell and the owners.

176

Bell's design is highly theatrical. The house and its grand staircase are reflected in the black-tiled swimming pool.

[ABOVE] *A lightning rod was essential for an iron house in an area prone to storms. Bell solved the problem with a copper pyramid which caps the roof.*

[RIGHT] *The block is a difficult one, the land falling away from front to back and from left to right. Bell used the earth removed during the construction of the dam to create a platform for the house to sit on.*

[ABOVE] *White timber frames and squares of carpeting define the living areas.*

[BELOW] *Gas-fired hot-water pipes beneath the floor provide central heating, but no country house is complete without a grand fireplace. Bell designed this one in a central brick pier, serving both the living and the dining areas.*

[ABOVE] *Beyond the brick courtyard is a self-contained guest house. The building also incorporates the garages and storage areas.*

[BELOW] *The kitchen occupies one of the four corners of the house. A double row of cupboards on the far wall conceals superb pots and pans in black metal.*

[ABOVE] *A feature of Bell's streamlined design is the pairs of sliding doors. The outer aluminium louvres, painted an unobtrusive white, provide security.*

[BELOW] *The design capitalizes on the breezes rolling in across the land.*

Bell was not interested in selecting paintings for the interior of the house. He believes that the views are the finest works of art.

The architect has used traditional materials to
create something beautifully unique.

PHOENIX RISING

Despite its Tuscan appearance, the inspiration for Sanders Wood in Victoria's Macedon Ranges came from the chicken house at Connorville, one of Tasmania's proudest heritage properties.

Designed by Richard Petersen in 1984 as a replacement for a house destroyed in the cataclysmic Ash Wednesday bushfires, it sits amid green lawns and enormous trees, including eucalypts and blackwoods. Just one room wide, with a cupola-topped central tower, the building belies its youthful brick construction. It is essentially a country house, a seasonal house, where sunshine and shadows leave a gentle imprint on the interior, with its mixture of Australian and European furnishings.

Precious pieces rescued from the fire include a pair of cast-iron garden wolves, the only survivors from a neighbouring property, and a painting of a woman peeling figs by Australian artist A. M. E. Bale from the owner's earlier home.

Close to the house, the garden is contained and strongly architectural, in no way competing with the large-scale trees and paddocks beyond. Annuals spill over from garden beds, and flowering vines climb walls. A faded blue pushcart displays yet more lavender, and a small dovecote dominates the centre of the herb garden.

[ABOVE] *A render of Colortex, applied with pebbles wrapped up in football socks, provided an aged look to the facade, which was then ruled to resemble blocks of sandstone.*

[LEFT] *Lush green paddocks run down to a creek on the property.*

[OPPOSITE PAGE] *The house sits amid green lawns and giant eucalyptus trees in Victoria's Macedon Ranges.*

[OPPOSITE PAGE, ABOVE LEFT] *A large fireplace contains a roaring log fire—a necessity during the winter months in the cold mountain climate. Above hangs a painting by Australian artist A. M. E. Bale, rescued from the Ash Wednesday fires.*

[OPPOSITE PAGE, BELOW LEFT] *A circular window in the bathroom lets in a gentle light.*

[OPPOSITE PAGE, BELOW RIGHT] *Warm colours create a comfortable atmosphere.*

[THIS PAGE AND OPPOSITE PAGE, ABOVE RIGHT] *A recent acquisition is this very Australian chandelier hanging from the vaulted ceiling in the dining room, a shower of copper and tin gum leaves designed by Canberra artist Ingrid Ping Davis.*

[ABOVE, LEFT] *The use of warm hues and natural timber bestows a serenity on Sanders Wood.*

[ABOVE, CENTRE] *Cuttings of lavender, a pair of well-worn gloves, rakes and boots proclaim this house as a gardener's home.*

[ABOVE, RIGHT] *A closer inspection of the work table reveals the day's harvest: a handful of cherry tomatoes.*

[RIGHT] *Lavender spills from a faded blue pushcart.*

These cast-iron wolves were rescued from the devastating Ash Wednesday fires, the only surviving possessions from a neighbouring property.

The garden of Sanders Wood is contained and highly architectural.

OLD MILL STILL AT WORK

Rising dramatically above the surrounding countryside, this old steam-driven flour mill on the coast of South Australia has been transformed into a comfortable country home for Christopher Norris of Country Style Interiors.

The mill is built of local bluestone and granite, the walls supported by huge pit-sawn blue and red gum beams, the floors a honey-coloured Baltic pine. Ground-floor walls are painted a soft blue, their rough texture creating a backdrop for antique and reproduction country furniture.

The mezzanine bedroom is straight out of a French farmhouse, with huge pit-sawn beams of the old mill complemented by a hand-forged wrought-iron bed and an antique rocking chair and side table.

Anxious to retain a rural working environment, Mr Norris was just as careful with the outdoor areas. A tumble of ruined walls, a pond, and a vegetable garden with farm implements and speckled chickens create a European country scene, while an avenue of forty-year-old cocos palms transported from Adelaide soften the tall, austere facade of the building and place it firmly on the Australian coastline.

Old brickwork frames the double door arch outside the kitchen, blending into the bluestone and granite walls of the mill.

[LEFT] *A lush, well-tended South Australian lawn brushes up against the time-etched stones of the garden wall.*

[FAR LEFT] *Speckled chickens and old farm implements are part of the mill's country character, complete with tumble-down walls, a pond and a vegetable garden.*

[BELOW] *Built in about 1850, the old South Australian mill is a combination of bluestone and granite walls, with pit-sawn red and blue gum beams.*

189

[RIGHT] *The kitchen has been divided from the dining area by a central workbench, and opens directly onto the garden. Hanging utensils and a range of kitchen collectables reinforce the country theme.*

[FAR RIGHT AND BELOW] *Downstairs, the living, dining and kitchen areas are finished in a deep robin's egg blue. All furniture was made by Country Style, including the bookcase, circular table, coffee table and chiffre. One exception: the collection of mortars and pestles rests atop a cantilevered mahogany wall cabinet from an old chemist's shop.*

[OPPOSITE PAGE] *The bedroom brings together the rustic elements of oregon floors and pit-sawn beams with a variety of antiques and antique-style additions from Chris Norris's company, Country Style Interiors. The hand-forged bed was made by Geoff Barnes, the provincial-style armoire is from Country Style, and the rocking chair, side table and cotton rug are by Thomas Woodard.*

THE WAY WE ARE

Sheila Carroll and her artist partner, Dennis Allard, have deliberately chosen to live the life of early colonial bush settlers. Their home, Ilford House, in New South Wales, has changed little from the original stone and timber structure built in 1868.

Probably the homestead for a small farm, Ilford House had been long abandoned and was facing demolition when discovered eighteen years ago by the present owners. Although anxious to preserve the original feeling, they were forced for safety's sake to make a few repairs: replace the white-ant-infested hall floor; install lights in the bedrooms upstairs; and remove the crumbling sandstone from the rear courtyard. Apart from these minor alterations, the house remains untouched. Cracked walls retain their original paint, the odd pane is missing from the dormer windows, and the wear and tear of more than a century of living has gone unchecked.

[ABOVE] *The family's boots, in various shapes and sizes, are clustered around an old dresser on the verandah.*

[RIGHT] *Behind the kitchen, a covered outroom provides catch-all space for assorted grinders and kerosene lanterns and a workbench, together with additional overhead drying racks for flowers.*

[FAR RIGHT] *Ilford House looks much as it would have when built in 1868.*

[OPPOSITE PAGE] *Old furniture from the Rylstone district is housed in the dim recesses of a corrugated-iron shed.*

[ABOVE] *A trio of vintage Australian chairs. Behind, an old bush dresser holds an engaging clutter of miscellanea.*

[LEFT] *The dormer window of this attic bedroom has most of its original panes.*

[FAR LEFT] *The hallway features the original paintwork and floorboards.*

[OPPOSITE PAGE] *In traditional colonial fashion, a massive antiquated fuel stove is used for cooking. Cast-iron pots, cauldrons, frying pans and a large hot-water urn make up Ilford's bush batterie de cuisine.*

A GENTLEMAN'S RESIDENCE

In 1885 Thomas Manifold, a young bachelor of Victoria's Western District, commissioned the building of a country residence. Designed by architect Albert Purchas, Wiridgil was a gentleman's house, a low-spreading sprawl of large rooms and wide hallways.

Clive Lucas, Australia's foremost conservation architect, has described Wiridgil as "Georgian Survival". Although the house incorporates many features typical of the late Victorian era, including symmetical verandahs and the Italianate detailing on the brick exterior, it is essentially Georgian in design. The main block of the house is balanced on either side by pavilions, one containing the billiard room, the other having the bedrooms. It is built of grey basalt bricks, common in the Western District, with contrasting cornerstones. The grand corrugated-iron roof is typical of many Australian homesteads.

Thomas's brother, Edward, inherited the house in 1895 and made further improvements to it: a grand dining room, a billiard room and a living hall which incorporated the original dining room, the front hall and a cross-passage.

[RIGHT] *Wiridgil features a symmetrical verandah, which runs the length of the eight-room house front.*

[BELOW] *A leafy wistaria hangs over the verandah's cast-iron frame, providing some shelter from the harsh Australian sunlight.*

[ABOVE, LEFT] *The cool tiled verandah of the homestead.*

[ABOVE, RIGHT] *When the original owner's brother inherited Wiridgil in 1895, he commissioned a number of additions to the house, including the billiard room.*

[RIGHT] *The Edwardian-style dining room is another of Edward's additions.*

The original dining room, front hall and cross-passage were combined to create this impressive living hall.

AN AUSTRALIAN THOROUGHBRED

There's a sense of heritage and timelessness about Rosebank, the classic centrepiece of a sheep and cattle property in the Adelaide Hills. Built in 1880 by George Melrose, the homestead has been owned and cared for by his heirs ever since. Now the home of Angus and Sylvia McLachlan, Rosebank was designed for large-scale country entertaining, with staff quarters and plenty of bedrooms for the coach parties that came every weekend.

Over the years it has been extended, rearranged and redecorated. Today, while the classic proportions and character remain intact, new bay windows allow sunshine into the family living room, where it reflects off pale glazed walls and ceilings. Elsewhere, small stained glass windows have been replaced with clear glazing, and dark timbers limed to resemble pine, oak and elm.

Horses are very much part of the Rosebank scene. Polo ponies are housed in magnificent stables close to the homestead.

200

[ABOVE] *Looking at Rosebank's main house from the front. Built in 1860, the house has been extended in the intervening years, but the classic homestead proportions of the facade remain intact.*

[RIGHT] *Equestrienne Sylvia McLachlan gives one of her ponies a morning hose-down.*

[OPPOSITE PAGE] *Beneath the back verandah hang assorted Drizabone coats and Akubra hats.*

[LEFT, TOP] *A side gate, opening onto an old birdhouse.*

[LEFT, CENTRE] *An antique stone ball and post half-shrouded in overgrowth.*

[LEFT, BELOW] *South Australian stone and corrugated-iron roofing were traditionally used in this part of the country for homesteads and their outbuildings.*

[RIGHT, TOP] *New colonial-style windows replaced the original small stained-glass windows in the living room.*

[RIGHT, CENTRE] *An old carved stone well, with beast spout.*

[RIGHT, BELOW] *A shady, summer-house-style retreat in the homestead gardens at Rosebank.*

[ABOVE] *The 131-year-old stone facade of Rosebank, with tessellated tile apron leading to the front door: the traditional homestead verandah.*

[LEFT] *Outdoor living at Rosebank goes beyond riding, with plenty of open-air entertaining space. Consistent with the vintage of the house, tables and benches are country-style, with old timbers and a well-weathered pergola.*

[FAR LEFT] *Jodhpur boots, rubber field boots, and footballs are neatly paired to one side of the front door.*

THE WILKINSON CONNECTION

Sprawled beneath the Monaro hills in southern New South Wales, Micalago Station has a twofold historical significance. It has been in the Ryrie family since 1839 and is one of the few houses ever to be renovated by one of Australia's greatest architects, the late Professor Leslie Wilkinson.

An important colonial family, the Ryries successfully combined political and military careers with running an outback property. Each generation renovated the house as the fancy took them, adding a dining room here, leaving a space there. When the late Jamie Ryrie and his wife, Elizabeth, went to live there in 1946, they called in Professor Wilkinson to give the haphazard collection of rooms and outbuildings cohesion. Wilkinson used shady verandahs to link the original slab dwelling with various unplanned additions which had been built over a hundred years.

Elizabeth Ryrie still lives here, with her collection of paintings, books, war medals and family portraits. Her special domain is the garden. "You get what you can, not necessarily what you want," is her attitude to country gardening in Australia. "You cope with the harsh elements, building shelter for delicate plants as you go."

205

[LEFT] *Micalago's sprawl of buildings sits at the foot of the Monaro Hills, not far from Canberra.*

[BELOW] *The name of the property was chosen by the original owners, the Rossi family. Count Rossi came to Australia in the 1820s as part of the Anglo-Corsican regiment.*

Long rows of poplars planted in the English tradition as a windbreak cast deep shadows in the Australian sunlight.

[ABOVE] *Beyond the horizon the rolling hills of Monaro country fold into the rugged terrain of the Snowy Mountains.*

[RIGHT] *Renovations carried out by Professor Wilkinson unified a hundred years of haphazard additions with shady verandahs and a Mediterranean-look exterior, which came to be known as Spanish Mission style.*

[TOP] *Wilkinson's additions (at left) created sheltered gardens shaded by large leafy trees.*

[ABOVE] *One of the original buildings, built by Count Rossi and constructed from large, irregular blocks of stone. In places, the walls are up to a metre thick.*

The grounds of Micalago offer new delights at every turn. This natural pond is nestled amongst willows, in sight of the house.

[TOP] *Wilkinson and the mistress of the house argued about the colour scheme of the exterior. Mrs Ryrie won the argument, and the house was painted white with a lilac-grey roof, a choice that complements the estate's English cottage-style garden.*

[ABOVE] *No nails were used in the construction of the shearing shed. Timber joints secure the entire structure.*

[TOP] *The woolshed, like the shearing shed, was originally covered by bark. Over the years the timber structures have been updated, first with a covering of timber shingles and more recently with galvanized iron.*

[ABOVE] *Like most Australian homesteads, Micalago makes good use of galvanized iron throughout the estate. The present owner believes that the iron of the roof was rolled in sheets on the property.*

[ABOVE] *Shady verandahs, shuttered windows and protected courtyards characterize Wilkinson's work.*

[LEFT] *The living areas are furnished with comfortable armchairs and sofas.*

[ABOVE] *Red silk wallpaper accentuates the grandeur of an eighteenth-century dining table, and a pair of cedar-panelled doors leads into the living room beyond.*

[RIGHT] *A portrait of Mrs Barrel by Sir Peter Lely hangs in the dining room.*

The Ryrie family holds a prominent place in the history of the colony. A collection of war medals dates back to the military career of Sir Granville Ryrie, who was made a major-general in 1919 and was Acting Minister of Defence in 1919–23.

[ABOVE] *Micalago has accumulated a fascinating collection of family heirlooms. The study is crammed with unexpected treasures, including a bust of the late James Ryrie.*

[LEFT] *Sir Granville's grandfather fought in the Battle of Waterloo.*

Coochin Coochin sits at the foot of the Minto crags in southern Queensland.

TROPICAL GEORGIAN

Typical of its time and place, Coochin Coochin, in southern Queensland, is a tropical version of the verandah-surrounded Georgian houses built throughout the colonies in the nineteenth century. It began life in 1845 as a low cedar-walled cottage with a shingle roof, comprising four rooms, all opening to the verandah. The kitchen was in a separate building at the back — a common fire precaution, as cooking on wood stoves was risky, and kitchen fires were not unusual. With water a scarce commodity and fire-fighting equipment nonexistent, a natural firebreak between the kitchen and the main house was considered almost essential.

Owned by the Bell family since 1883, the small house has been extended and renovated haphazardly until there are now seven bedrooms under four separate rooflines, connected only by verandahs and external covered walkways.

The verandahs are important to the lifestyle of Coochin Coochin's present incumbents, Tim and Jane Bell. Summer and winter, most activities take place in these wide and shady places. They provide a perfect escape from the heat, their adjustable timber shutters and canvas blinds controlling early-morning and late-afternoon sun. The family eat here, relax here, do business and entertain here.

Almost untouched since the 1840s, the walls and low ceiling of the sitting room are panelled in local cedar, the rich red of the timber blending perfectly with early Australian furniture.

[ABOVE] *Wistaria thrives in this subtropical climate and brings an enchanting fall of mauve blossoms to the garden.*

[LEFT] *The property is one of the most prosperous stations in an area blessed with ample rainfall. The years of good fortune have allowed the owners to spend time on nurturing a delightful garden.*

[RIGHT] *Canvas blinds on the homestead's wide verandahs keep out the heat of the late-afternoon sun.*

[BELOW, LEFT] *Timber louvres provide ventilation while keeping out the sun.*

[BELOW, RIGHT] *Rooms were added to the homestead in a haphazard manner over the years. External covered walkways link the various sections of the house.*

The original structure, built in 1845, was a
humble four-room house with a shingle roof.
Today the house encompasses seven bedrooms,
and the timber shingles have been covered by
corrugated iron.

The "squatter's chair" in the foreground was designed with extended arms, allowing the sitter to rest with his feet up on them after a hard day's work on the land.

The original structure of the house still stands, with four rooms opening onto a low-slung verandah. The present owners have used Aboriginal artefacts to decorate their home. Ironically, the site of the homestead was chosen to provide a strategic surveillance point against attack from local Aborigines.

[LEFT] *When the original homestead was built in 1845, local red cedar was used for interior panelling. Almost 150 years later, the panelling in the sitting room is still beautiful.*

[BELOW] *The highly polished cedar complements the early Australian furniture.*

THE HOMESTEAD VILLAGE

The original house of Woolmers was no more than a weatherboard bungalow, built by Thomas Archer on the banks of Tasmania's South Esk River in 1818. It was not until many years later that the homestead was extended and aggrandized under the direction of Thomas's son, William, the first Tasmanian-born architect. William updated Woolmers with an Italian villa front, which gave the house a sweeping front hall, a dining room and a handsome drawing room. William's alterations also included a garden design incorporating handsome gateways, a fountain and a smoking pavilion.

Australian homesteads often resemble small towns — Woolmers, for example, has several estate cottages. The outbuildings represent various stages in the history of the property and reflect the stylistic norms of those periods. The gardener's house is an ornate cottage in the English style. The symmetrical structure of the stables and coach-house, built in 1847, is typical of the Georgian tradition. A weatherboard woolshed, built from local hardwood, is thought to be the oldest in Australia. It is certainly the oldest building on the property, dating back to 1815, three years before the original residence was built.

Perhaps it is a result of Tasmania's isolation that the house and its furnishing have withstood the passing of fashion. Much of the original oak, rosewood and mahogany furniture survives, as do the gilt cornice poles and curtains of the drawing room.

Like many early Australian homesteads, Woolmers was a self-contained, self-sufficient "village" made up of several buildings, each with its own specific purpose — buttery, slaughterhouse, lodge, gardener's cottage and so forth. Outbuildings were added to the property over a number of years, each building not a new component of one unified style but a reflection of the architectural fashions of its own particular period.

[ABOVE] *The Italian villa front of Woolmers, designed by the owner's son, William Archer.*

[RIGHT] *The original verandahed weatherboard house built by Thomas Archer in 1818. The kitchen block, with its two large chimneys, was added in 1847.*

[ABOVE, LEFT] *Much of the original furniture survives, making the house a valuable and fascinating example of an early Victorian home. Oak furniture in the front hall was chosen by William Archer in the 1840s.*

[ABOVE, RIGHT] *Curved doors lead off the centre hall into the service passage behind the dining room.*

[LEFT] *The red flock wallpaper of the dining room was hung in 1859. Blind arches contain original pieces of mahogany furniture.*

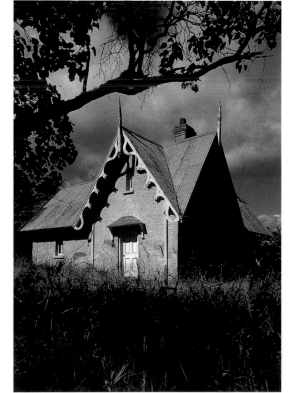

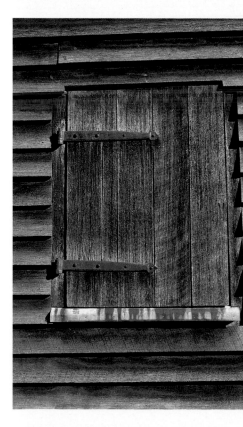

[ABOVE, LEFT] *Changing architectural fashions throughout Woolmers' long history are recorded in the property's diverse collection of buildings. This two-storey building displays the symmetrical structure typical of the Georgian period, while elsewhere on the property an estate lodge bears the influence of the popular Gothic revival.*

[LEFT] *Hung on hand-forged straps, the window shutters of the woolshed have withstood the elements for more than 150 years.*

[FAR LEFT] *The steeply gabled gardener's cottage, nestled on the banks of the South Esk River, is an example of a cottage ornée.*

225

Built in 1815, Woolmers' weatherboard woolshed is thought to be the oldest in Australia.

ALONG THE TROPICAL COASTLINE and in the dry, dusty centre of the state, Queensland style is dictated by the environment, particularly the ever-present heat. The demand for housing with plenty of shaded areas and good ventilation meant that, almost from the beginning of European settlement, builders created architectural "sunscreens" for houses — deep verandahs, a tracery of lattice, and the angular slats of louvres — which became the basis of a distinctive Queensland style.

Tasmania's colder climate demanded no such architectural necessities. As in America's New England, Anglo-European style ruled here, with a predilection shown for Georgian features. The verandah, that icon of Australian style, was not used as a matter of course; where it does appear it is usually shallow and almost purely ornamental.

While the grand estates of Queensland, with their wide verandahs and decorative elements of ventilation, fascinate, Tasmania boasts equally grand and surprisingly sophisticated examples of nineteenth-century architectural fashions: neo-Classical revival detailing, Gothic-style exteriors, and influences of Italianate style and Irish architecture. On a smaller but no less interesting scale, many farmhouses and their furnishings have survived the passing of the years. The structures of houses left empty for decades remain intact, their durability a legacy of their sturdy stone and timber construction and the absence of the corrosive humidity that has taken its toll on their counterparts to the north.

FT] *A veil of lattice* *s been drawn over this* *eensland house to* *tect it from the fierce* *thern sun.*

THE FAR NORTH

In the typical Queensland house, timber lattice and louvres enclose deep verandahs, discouraging the harsh sunlight without hindering the flow of air. These semi-enclosed verandahs became additional living spaces and occasional sleeping areas when the heat inside the house, trapped under a corrugated-iron roof, became unbearable.

Beneath the houses, the cavities created by stumps and stilts still deter snakes and protect the house from flood, but they too have evolved in use and height to become a hanging space for laundry in the wet season — and secret cubby-houses for generations of Australian children.

Wide verandahs, lattice, louvres and window hoods have been essential elements of Queensland design almost from the early days of settlement, but over the years these utilitarian elements have evolved into ornate and adventurous features, with simple panelling replaced by striking architectural geometries and patterning. Even the humble little window hoods made of galvanized iron or timber acquired their own embellishments of scalloped borders and decorative cut-outs.

SUNSCREENED SYMMETRY

Wylarah is a U-shaped building with a verandah running along the three sides of the house and across the open top of the U. The northern end features a central bell flèche, while the glazed windows of the southern gables shed light on the large multipurpose area occupying the centre of the structure.

The detail of Wylarah's timber walls is remarkable: cypress pine boards are laid horizontally and vertically across lengths of ironbark to create an unusual panelling effect. While the house has many typically Queensland characteristics, the influence of the English Gothic revival is to be seen in the Tudor-look panelling and the large central room.

[TOP, LEFT] *Windows set into the southern gables allow light into the central living room.*

[TOP, RIGHT] *The combined living room, dining room and study is an Australian version of the "great hall".*

[ABOVE, LEFT] *Both interior and exterior walls have been left unpainted to expose the remarkable timberwork.*

[ABOVE, CENTRE] *The house is raised on stumps to hold it high above flood waters.*

[ABOVE, RIGHT] *The entrance porch, in the south wall, belongs unmistakably to a country homestead.*

THE VERANDAHED PAVILION

Built at the turn of the century in southeastern Queensland, Wyaralong is another typically northern house. The detail of the verandah, including a dowelled balustrade with gates at the top of each set of stairs, gives it a lightness of structure unusual even among tropical houses.

Set high off the ground, the house is a collection of pavilions linked by verandahs. The modest interiors are characteristic of Queensland houses built in the late Victorian era, in marked contrast to the much more ornate interiors of the south.

[TOP, LEFT] *The house is framed by a pair of enormous palm trees.*

[TOP, RIGHT] *The bedroom pavilion was a later addition, but the owners took care to replicate the late Victorian detail of the original verandah.*

[ABOVE, LEFT] *The unadorned interiors, painted eau-de-Nil green, are typical of Queensland houses of this period.*

[ABOVE, CENTRE] *The narrow hall leads directly to the dining room, the only room in the house with a fireplace.*

[ABOVE, RIGHT] *The verandahs linking the pavilions are sheltered by a convex roof independent of the main roof.*

THE DEEP SOUTH

Cultivated in the lower latitudes of Australia's southern island-state, Tasmanian design offers cottages, farmhouses and grand estates influenced by a cool climate. The stone and brick facades of cottages in Hobart's Battery Point survive as examples of fine craftsmanship and Georgian characteristics undisguised by an add-on verandah, while semi-circular fanlights, neo-Classical architecture, English barns and cold-climate gardens speak eloquently of old memories enshrined in a new world.

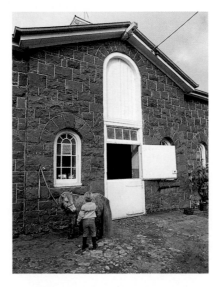

A RURAL ELEGANCE

The Italianate influence that was to become popular during the early Victorian period was incorporated into the design of Bicton, a two-storeyed country house built in Tasmania in 1837. The brick and stone facade of the house, along with features such as the principal chimneypieces, have a distinctive Italianate character. In contrast, the stables and coach-houses behind the house have typically Georgian exteriors.

[TOP, LEFT] *The sophisticated design of Bicton belies its rural location.*

[TOP, RIGHT] *Fitted cupboards stand on either side of the fireplace in the dining room.*

[ABOVE, LEFT] *The stables and coach-houses have the characteristic utilitarian exteriors of Georgian architecture.*

[ABOVE, RIGHT] *A delightful feature of the stables is elaborately carved woodwork.*

GRAND GEORGIAN

A sweeping gravel drive leads to Killymoon, an estate of grand Georgian design built in 1842. Standing two storeys high atop an elevation formed by a terrace wall, the house looks out across river flats in the Tasmanian countryside. The kitchen and several offices are housed in the basement.

Killymoon's stately ashlar facades are balanced at either side by brick walls enclosing the kitchen garden and a flower garden. The front hall is dominated by an imperial staircase, which leads upwards to the chamber floor and downwards to the basement. The dining and sitting rooms feature bowed ends and tripartite window structures.

[TOP, LEFT] *The grand sweep of Killymoon's tall facades is offset by rambling gardens on either side of the house.*

[TOP, RIGHT] *In the dining room, the black marble chimneypiece reflects the Italianate influence of the period.*

[ABOVE, LEFT] *The estate features a charming Gothic-style coach-house.*

[ABOVE, RIGHT] *The basement formed by the elevation houses a large kitchen and a number of offices.*

BEYOND THEIR COASTAL CITIES AND regional towns, Australians have a vast backyard to play in. From the silky turquoise waters of Queensland's Great Barrier Reef and the emerald ocean off Western Australia to the sunburnt outback and the eastern snowfields, the playgrounds of Australia each have their own character and their own expressions of style.

The tourist boom of the affluent 1980s brought a new imperative of style to the coastal and island holiday spots inside the Barrier Reef, generating ever more sumptuous resorts that paid a nodding architectural acknowledgment to traditional tropical Queensland elements — some on a surreal scale of lavishness that owed more of a debt to Hawaii or the Caribbean than to Airlie Beach. The Mirage at Port Douglas is one of the most pleasing examples of this combination of get-away fantasy and historical allusion.

Near Uluru, or Ayers Rock, in Australia's Dead Heart, the Yulara resort complex offers a civilized way to see another wonder of the world amid one of the most inhospitable terrains on earth. Like a ship in the ocean, the complex masters its desert environment without interfering with it.

For a country so dominated by sunshine, Australia's snowfields in New South Wales and Victoria are a skier's paradise from July to September. Chalets and lodges are the norm here, but newer versions such as those found at Dinner Plain are taking on a distinctly Australian flavour.

Far away from the chill of the mountains is the world's longest beach, in the town of Broome. Located in the remote far northwest of Australia, this old pearling town is growing into one of the country's more exotic tourist spots, and with the new interest has come the new Cable Beach resort, where upmarket bungalows are patterned faithfully after the bungalows of the pearling masters of yore.

[LEFT] *Seen against the pinks and mauves of a tropical sunset, the marina at the Mirage Port Douglas Resort takes on a dreamlike quality.*

A MIRAGE REALIZED

With the anticipated explosion in the number of international visitors in recent years, former sleepy holiday places inside the Great Barrier Reef and on the North Queensland coast have grown into luxury resorts, competing with each other to build bigger and better hotel complexes. The Mirage Port Douglas Resort is one such tropical fantasy. Set amid imported palm trees and manmade beaches, lagoons and waterfalls, it comprises a five-star hotel, a marina, a country club, villas, a sports complex and a championship golf course, all built on a reclaimed swamp.

Designed by Media Five Architects, the complex is clean, disciplined and simple. Working under government constraints requiring buildings to be in the North Queensland style and not to exceed the height of the tree-line, the architects opted for a crablike design, with two blocks of three-angled wings leading off a central lobby.

A spectacular saltwater lagoon covering more than 2 hectares encircles the main buildings, lapping the balconies of most ground-floor guest rooms. Public areas are furnished with antique pieces from Europe and Asia, while the 300 rooms and suites have a distinctly tropical ambience, with louvred shutters and ceiling fans.

240

[ABOVE AND RIGHT] *The villas look out towards the landscaped gardens and golf course of the resort's country club. Designed by Peter Thomson, the eighteen-hole championship course features a unique aquatic driving range.*

[ABOVE] *A wonderland interpretation of the North Queensland style, the Mirage is surrounded by a network of swimmable manmade saltwater lagoons. A major engineering triumph, these lagoons are complemented by waterfalls and "beaches" created with imported sand, together with densely planted gardens and lush pandanus palms that reinforce the sense of a tropical paradise.*

[LEFT] *White-jacketed waiters in the resort's restaurant ready themselves for the evening's guests.*

When night falls on the Mirage, the lagoons
are outlined in skeins of light, the ribbons
of illumination adding to the feeling of a
fantasy paradise.

PEARL AT THE EDGE OF THE OCEAN

Perched at the edge of the Kimberley ranges on the northwestern coastline, the sleepy nineteenth-century pearling town of Broome is emerging as one of Australia's most exotic destinations.

Today, camel treks, coastal safaris and the new Cable Beach resort provide the town with its main source of revenue, but the pearl trade is still plied here, and pearl emporiums tempt visitors with jewellery made from the local harvest.

Broome's multicultural history of colonial and Asian elements and its location near the tropics are reflected in its architecture. In the traditional Broome bungalow, exterior walls consist of louvred hopper awnings, which swing open from the bottom to welcome balmy breezes while deflecting the sun. The internal periphery of the house is used as a corridor-cum-enclosed verandah, with bedrooms set back in the cooler core.

[ABOVE] *The hallmark colours of the Broome coastline: red, gold and jade-blue.*

[RIGHT] *Camel trekkers at Cable Beach.*

[BELOW] *The Chinatown Markets offer a wealth of curiosities to browse through.*

[RIGHT AND BELOW] *The old Sun Picture Theatre on Carnarvon Street, Australia's last working outdoor "picture garden", where patrons watch the latest movie beneath the stars.*

[BOTTOM, RIGHT] *The passing of time has not registered in some parts of Broome, where sandy streets and corrugated iron houses are much as they were a century ago.*

A CAPTAIN'S COTTAGE

Once the pearling capital of the world, Broome has been shaped by its colonial past and by later arrivals from the East — the indentured workers from Asia and the Pacific islands who came to free-dive for pearls in the shallow coastal water. Particularly successful transplants were the Chinese, who settled here and became the town's shopkeepers, giving Broome a rich dollop of architectural spice along the way.

Surviving relics of Broome's boom past are many. The most famous is the cottage built for the town's best-known pearling master at the turn of the century, Captain Gregory. With wide verandahs enclosed by hopper windows and latticework, dark-stained jarrah floors, and cool interior sleeping spaces, it is typical of bungalows built in Broome at the turn of the century. Lord McAlpine, the British peer who has made Broome his home away from home, undertook the restoration of Captain Gregory's cottage for future generations to enjoy. At the same time he modelled the guest bungalows of his luxurious Cable Beach Club resort (see following pages) on the cottage for the current generation to enjoy today.

247

[THIS AND OPPOSITE PAGE] *With wide verandahs enclosed by hopper windows and latticework, dark-stained jarrah floors, and cool interior sleeping spaces, Captain Gregory's cottage is typical of bungalows built in Broome at the turn of the century.*

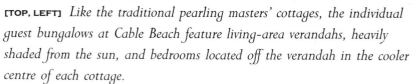

[TOP, LEFT] *Like the traditional pearling masters' cottages, the individual guest bungalows at Cable Beach feature living-area verandahs, heavily shaded from the sun, and bedrooms located off the verandah in the cooler centre of each cottage.*

[TOP, RIGHT] *The Chinese influence on Broome, dating back to the original pearl divers, is acknowledged in the design of the resort and its many rare artefacts from Asia.*

[ABOVE, LEFT] *One of the main buildings in the resort complex. It is heavily shielded from the sun and designed with high peaked ceilings to allow the hot Broome air to rise.*

[ABOVE, RIGHT] *The front of a typical private bungalow, complete with hopper awnings and latticed verandah.*

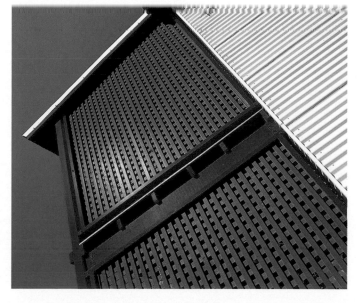

MODERN HISTORY

A luxury resort in a sleepy town at the edge of the wild Kimberley, Cable Beach Club is the brainchild of British peer Alistair McAlpine, who fell under the spell of Broome many years ago and made it his own, building himself a magnificent bush complex (and building the town an equally magnificent open air conservation zoo).

Lord McAlpine's vision was a five-star resort to draw visitors to the old pearling town, a resort with all the international trimmings, but created within the traditional architectural style of his beloved Broome. Following local examples such as the historic cottage of pearling master Captain Gregory, McAlpine's architects designed a series of guest bungalows along traditional lines, with wide verandahs and bedrooms located in the cool core of the cottages. The resort's main buildings are more contemporary tributes to the melting-pot colonial, Chinese and Malay culture of this old pearling town.

Faithful to the spirit of Captain Gregory and the Chinese immigrants who settled in the old pearling town, Lord McAlpine directed the architects to incorporate the deep verandahs, jarrah floors and traditional Chinese-cum-colonial colours of the old pearling masters' bungalows into the new Cable Beach resort.

DEAD HEART, HIGH DESIGN

Twenty kilometres from Uluru, or Ayers Rock, the sleek white mylar sails of Yulara Resort soar out of the barren outback landscape, distinct from the harsh spinifex and red-earth environment, yet in key with it.

Designed by Philip Cox, one of Australia's most highly regarded architects, Yulara was created to preserve this famous and fragile area from the corrosive effects of tourism, replacing the scattered motels and caravan parks with a single self-contained tourist "platform" that would attract visitors even while it preserved the very things they came to see.

The resort complex is built on a podium that removes it from direct contact with the land. The podium spine hugs the contours of the sand dune, becoming invisible from the next ridge. Atop the podium, the Four Seasons resort occupies one end of the spine and the five-star Sheraton Hotel the other. In between, a connecting village concourse of shops and diversions — protected from the ferocious outback sun by the white "sails" — provides the usual diversions of a major resort complex, together with a view like no other on earth.

250

[RIGHT] *The sinuous curve of the Yulara complex follows the line of an existing sand dune. Built on a podium, Yulara commands magnificent views of Ayers Rock and the stark Red Centre without interfering with the fragile bushflower-and-spinifex ecosystem of a "Dead Heart" that is very much alive.*

[ABOVE] *Like that of the Sydney Opera House, Yulara's brilliant design by architect Philip Cox lends itself to the photographer's imaginative eye. Here the complex is seen from above the promenades of "sails" that shield the resort's walkways from the ferocious Central Australian sunlight.*

[LEFT] *The complex seen from below the podium, finished in a baked-earth red that is in key with the landscape.*

[RIGHT] *Looking from the edge of the complex towards one of the three hotels in the resort.*

[FAR RIGHT] *Detail of the rigging for the tent-like sails that protect the open promenades from the sunlight.*

[BELOW] *After dark, the fierce brilliance of the sun is replaced by the inky blackness of the desert night. Light reflected off the complex's pool and surrounding buildings is caught in a bright blue-white wrap of the overhead sails.*

[ABOVE] *Bright and hardy Sturt Peas growing at the edge of the complex, a reminder of the varied and beautiful life forms that manage to thrive in this harsh environment.*

[LEFT] *In the Four Seasons Hotel, accommodation has been designed in the Australian vernacular, with bull-nosed verandahs and balconies echoing Victorian terrace houses.*

[FAR LEFT] *A promenade through the complex. Aboriginal art motifs, like the lizard seen at far right, recur throughout the resort.*

ALPINE AUSTRALIA

With its reputation for heat, dust, warm tropical waters and desert sands, Australia does not conjure up visions of snow-covered mountains. Admittedly, the season is short and not always reliable, but when the conditions are right the Australian alps offer great skiing — with a few exciting departures from the European norm, including cross-country trails that meander between ancient snow gums across some of the most spectacular scenery in the country.

Australian ski villages have an outback rather than a chalet theme, catering for year round visitors with horse riding and bushwalking facilities.

Among these, Dinner Plain alpine ski resort is special. Just 8 kilometres from Mount Hotham in Victoria, the resort is a planned alpine town which will eventually provide 2000 beds, housed in a spectacular-looking hotel and individually designed private lodges. The brainchild of Melbourne architect Peter McIntyre, it has won sixteen major architectural awards plus the Sir Zelman Cowen Award for outstanding design.

254

[ABOVE] *The stone and cedar gateway to the complex, complete with its own miniature corrugated-iron-covered verandah.*

[RIGHT] *All architectural aspects were strictly controlled by the developers, yet no two buildings are the same. Most are of stone and cedar construction, with arcs and angles, crooked chimney pipes, and steep snowproof roofs.*

[LEFT] *Mount Elizabeth House, one of the freehold mountain retreats in the complex. Soft-smudge finishes and natural building materials allow these virtually brand-new houses to blend in with the landscape as if they have been here for a century.*

[BELOW, LEFT] *Alpine Australia after an early snowfall, with gum trees standing in a blanket of powder snow.*

[BELOW] *Foard's Lodge, a 20-suite guesthouse in the village.*

[ABOVE] *Massive beams and thick treetrunks support the mezzanine and roof of The Pub, Dinner Plain's central* après ski *spot.*

[RIGHT] *Stone, cedar and snow — key ingredients of the Dinner Plains design, both architectural and heaven-sent.*

[FAR RIGHT] *Houses have been fitted out with total comfort in mind. Here, a steaming hot shower or bath can be enjoyed while gazing out to the snow-frosted surroundings outside.*

[ABOVE] Exchanging ski parkas for oilskins, a group of early-morning riders and their mounts pause at a mountain stream, where the current moves swiftly enough to keep the thin layer of ice broken into small floes.

[RIGHT] Snow-tolerant gum trees, Eucalyptus pauciflora, grow exclusively in the Australian alps.

THE MANY INFLUENCES OF AUSTRALIA'S multicultural population come to bear on the shape and style of the country's restaurants. The traditional characteristics of old English dining rooms, European cafés and bistros, and New York brasseries, are reworked to accommodate the temperament of Australian dining.

In the cities, urbane bistros reflect the sophisticated nature of chic city dining. Styles often mirror the character of the cities themselves: the intricate inlaid flooring of many Melbourne establishments is a metaphor for that city's cultural influences; the light and spacious rooms of Sydney restaurants capture the mood of alfresco dining, even when the sun doesn't shine.

The best of these restaurants represent the leading edge of Australian architecture. Restaurants, bistros and cafés allow interior designers a creative freedom that cannot be matched in a domestic residence. The interiors of these establishments sometimes approach the realm of fantasy, the creations of some of Australia's most dynamic imaginations. At other times, tiled floors, dark bentwood chairs and hard, almost industrial surfaces create a "drop dead" environment for chic 1990s dining.

Moving away from the heart of town, restaurants overlooking Australia's waterways and beaches make a feature of their surroundings. The innovative architecture of these restaurants encompasses the land, working with both the natural beauty and the inherent awkwardness of their location.

[LEFT] *Melbourne after dark: Pieroni's restaurant in Toorak Road.*

259

BATHERS PAVILION

As its name suggests, the Bathers Pavilion restaurant occupies what were once the changing sheds at Sydney's Balmoral Beach. Recent years had already seen the conversion of the old pavilion into a restaurant called Mischa's, but the new proprietor, Victoria Alexander, initiated some significant changes to the existing building when she took over. Central to these was the removal of internal arches to form an uninterrupted flow of space. Architect Alex Popov designed the restaurant's pivoting glass windows, which allow generous views of the beach and capitalize on ocean breezes. At the entrance bar, wooden louvres serve a similar purpose.

Sand and sea colours set off against floors of polished concrete and white-washed walls create what Victoria has called "Santa Fe with beach overtones", a theme reinforced by an eclectic selection of Australian furniture and witty table displays of vegetables, starfish, bowls of fruit, and cactuses in terracotta pots.

The weathered timber of old furniture such as an open-shelf dresser built in the 1890s and a shearers' worktable create a subdued interior, so that the emphasis is on the view of Balmoral Beach. The blues and greens of painted surfaces echo the colours outside.

260

[ABOVE] *White tablecloths and bentwood chairs create an atmosphere of "beach casual".*

[RIGHT] *The pivotal glass windows were designed by Alex Popov.*

*The beachfront location of Bathers Pavilion is
one of Sydney's most glorious sites.*

[ABOVE, LEFT] *An open-shelf dresser on the right complements the muted tones of whitewashed walls and faded Kelim rugs.*

[ABOVE, RIGHT] *Witty touches such as displays of raw vegetables in old country-style containers offset the subdued atmosphere of the interior.*

[OPPOSITE PAGE, ABOVE] *Timber louvres give the option of an enclosed room or a free-flowing space.*

[BELOW, LEFT] *Lilies adorn the old shearers' table. Made from Kauri pine and oregon, the table was found in Mudgee.*

[BELOW, CENTRE] *The restaurant's proprietor, Victoria Alexander, has described the style of food as "eclectic and very Australian".*

[BELOW, RIGHT] *Placed within easy reach on a side table, herbs and condiments add visual flavour to the interior.*

BEROWRA WATERS INN

Gay Bilson's Berowra Waters Inn sits almost in camouflage on a bank of the Hawkesbury River, so well does architect Glenn Murcutt's design respond to the natural surroundings.

The restaurant makes a feature of its secluded location. Access is by ferry from Berowra Waters wharf — or by seaplane, for the more adventurous. Guests alight at the restaurant jetty, which leads directly into a small stone entrance built down at the river's edge. A flight of stairs then takes them to the main dining room. The floor space of the dining area is long and narrow, ensuring that every table has a river view.

The design downplays the presence of structure. Glass louvres lining one entire side of the restaurant create the illusion of a three-walled space, completely open on the river side. The flow of breezes through the louvres and the spacious layout of tables enhance the feeling of open-air dining. Downstairs at river level, bare sandstone walls and coir matting recall the colours of clay riverbeds.

[ABOVE AND OPPOSITE PAGE] *A wall of glass louvres opens the restaurant to views of Berowra Waters. The restaurant is accessible by ferry or seaplane.*

[RIGHT] *The sandstone entrance is a remnant of the original building on the site.*

[ABOVE] *A central bar with giant maplewood core. On the other side of the bar, glass display cases hold tempting arrays of desserts.*

[RIGHT] *Looking down the staircase from the main dining area.*

[LEFT] *The vast expanse of walls in the old warehouse were given a special faux marble treatment by artist Nicholas Register.*

[BELOW] *The old sawtooth ceiling of the original clothing warehouse was left intact. Scallop mosaics, three-dimensional patterns of tiles, and border patterns break up the interior space into seating clusters and traffic "streets".*

ROSATI

Like Parisians, Melburnians take style very seriously, and when it comes to fashion, food and design, their countrymen in the other capital cities generally concede that Melbourne is at the leading edge.

At Rosati, all three elements of good living come together, largely thanks to owner Piero Gesualdi. The man behind the stylish Mason's boutiques, Mr Gesualdi has brought his fashion sense—and a background in architecture—to bear on this, his first restaurant.

Created within the shell of a former clothing warehouse, Rosati is European-style high design in a low-tech Australian building. Under a sawtoothed industrial roof, vast sweeps of elegant mosaic and tilework, faux marble panels, and timber tub chairs in Philippe Starck style, have been brought together in what Mr Gesualdi has called "contemporary classic".

267

CHECKPOINT CHARLIE

This Melbourne nightclub takes its "East meets West" design cues from Cold War Berlin and the post-apocalyptic sets of *Blade Runner*, welded together in a crumbling, classical-industrial interior which architect Peter Brown calls neo-Fundamentalist.

Selected architectural elements were torn out of context and reassembled abstractly. Out of this constructive destruction emerges a visual opulence, a richness of texture and form that is both strange and stimulating.

Distressed paintwork and raw classical detailing, ripped apart and reconstructed, and equally raw Industrial elements of milled steel and aluminium have been used to create distinct areas of activity in the nightclub, moving from a deconstructed classical lower-level dance floor to the industrial-style mezzanine restaurant level.

Linking the two spaces is a milled-steel staircase that takes its form from pre-war Europe and its substance from post-war industry. It is, as the architect says, a singularly appropriate design ingredient for a nightclub.

268

[THIS PAGE] *Milled steel was used for the staircase, this raw industrial material offset with ravaged classical detailing. Rough fresco walls and industrial-age chairs reinforce the crumbling fantasy setting. Russian signage and roughed-up decor project the "East meets West" theme of the nightclub's name.*

[OPPOSITE PAGE] *The jagged window design at the bottom of the staircase suggests a bombed-out building.*

An old South Australian packing-case cupboard is used to store red wine at Bathers Pavilion restaurant.